CUYAHOGA COUNTY

and Greater Cleveland

The Cleveland skyline illuminates the night, casting a reflection on the Cuyahoga River.

CUYAHOGA COUNTY

and Greater Cleveland

Tina G. Rubin and Linda Chase

Acknowledgements

This book was produced in cooperation with Cuyahoga County, Ohio. Cherbo Publishing Group gratefully acknowledges its important contribution to *Cuyahoga County and Greater Cleveland*.

 cherbo publishing group, inc.

Cherbo Publishing Group, Inc.
Encino, California 91316
© 2011 by Cherbo Publishing Group, Inc.
All rights reserved. Published 2011.

Printed in Canada
By Friesens

Subsidiary Production Office
Santa Rosa, CA, USA
888.340.6049

Library of Congress Cataloging-in-Publication data
Rubin, Tina G., and Chase, Linda
A pictorial guide highlighting Cuyahoga County's economic and social advantages.

Library of Congress Control Number:
2010937580
ISBN 978-1-882933-38-9
Visit the CPG Web site at
www.cherbopub.com.

president	JACK C. CHERBO
chief operating officer	ELAINE HOFFMAN
editorial director	LINDA CHASE
profiles writers	B. D. CAMPBELL
	TINA G. RUBIN
creative director	PERI A. HOLGUIN
senior designer	THEODORE E. YEAGER.
sales administrator	JOAN K. BAKER
client services supervisor	PATRICIA DE LEONARD
senior client services coordinator	LESLIE E. SHAW
administrative assistant	BILL WAY
eastern regional manager	MARCIA WEISS
publisher's representative	DON JOHNSON

The information in this publication is the most recent available and has been carefully researched to ensure accuracy. Cherbo Publishing Group, Inc. cannot and does not guarantee either the correctness of all information furnished it or the complete absence of errors, including omissions.

To purchase additional copies of this book, contact Joan Baker at Cherbo Publishing Group: jbaker@cherbopub.com or phone 818.783.0040 ext. 27.

TABLE OF CONTENTS

Whirlwind tour (from opposite page, left): Key Tower, Cleveland's tallest building; the exterior of storied Cleveland Browns Stadium; Victory Fountain, in front of

Fan fare (above from left): Dining alfresco at the Great Lakes Brewing Company; a Cleveland Indians player signs a ball for a fan before a ballgame at Progressive Field; the stalls at Westside Market offer baked goods, produce, meats, and other fresh foods.

Cleveland kalaidescope (from opposite page, left): Flamenco dancers perform at The Arcade; colorful costumes provide a dazzling spectacle at the Cleveland University Circle Parade; kids have a ball at the Great Lakes Science Center.

CORPORATIONS & ORGANIZATIONS PROFILED

The following organizations have made a valuable commitment to the quality of this publication.

BUSINESS VISIONARIES

The following companies and organizations are recognized as innovators in their fields and have played a prominent role in this publication, as they have in Cuyahoga County.

CBIZ, Inc.
6050 Oak Tree Boulevard South, Suite 500, Cleveland, OH 44131
Phone: 216-447-9000 / Fax: 216-447-9007
Web site: www.cbiz.com
NYSE: CBZ
"Our Business is Growing Yours"

ka Architecture
1468 West 9th Street, Suite 600, Cleveland, Ohio 44113
James B. Heller, President
Phone: 216-781-9144 / Fax: 216-781-6566
E-mail: jheller@kainc.com
Web site: www.kainc.com

Developers Diversified Realty Corporation
3300 Enterprise Parkway, Beachwood, OH 44122
Phone: 216-755-5500 or
(toll free) 877-225-5337 (877-CALL DDR)
Fax: 216-755-1500
Web site: www.ddr.com
"Owners, managers, and developers
of a dynamic international portfolio
of highly valued shopping centers"

KeyBank
127 Public Square, Cleveland, OH 44114
Phone (Consumers): 800-523-7248
Phone (Businesses): 888-539-4249
Web site: www.key.com

Dollar Bank
1301 East 9th Street, Cleveland, OH 44114
Andrew D. Devonshire, President, Dollar Bank Ohio
Phone: 216-736-7353
Web site: www.dollarbank.com

The PNC Financial Services Group, Inc.
1900 East 9th Street, Cleveland, OH 44114
Phone: 888-PNC-BANK
Web site: www.pnc.com

Holding a globe representing international economic activity, *Commerce* is poised alongside *Jurisprudence* above the old Federal Courthouse on Superior Avenue

FOREWORD

First-time visitors to Cuyahoga County are often amazed at how beautiful, vibrant, and livable our corner of the Midwest is, but those of us who live, work, raise families, and play here are well aware of the unparalleled treasures that make our region unique.

With the City of Cleveland at its center, Cuyahoga County is located on the south shore of Lake Erie at the mouth of the twisting Cuyahoga River and extends 20 miles east, west, and south. The county's treasure trove of sights and experiences is both evocative of the great urban centers of the East Coast and Europe and representative of the solid expansiveness and simplicity of America's heartland. With world-class architecture, art, and cultural institutions, and a colorful diversity of urban neighborhoods and idyllic villages interspersed with verdant hills and parks, Cuyahoga County is truly a shining American gem.

Once symbolic of America's industrial might, the region has taken a 21st-century global leadership role in health care, technology, sustainability, and innovation. As we embark on the next steps in our reinvention, our illustrious heritage, as well as the strength, passion, and determination of our hard-working populace, will be the pillars upon which our renaissance is founded. We invite everyone to share the rich promise that is Cuyahoga County.

TIMELINE

1796   1825   1845   1870

Moses Cleaveland

1796 Moses Cleaveland conducts a surveying party through the Connecticut Western Reserve. The group plots out a town along the Cuyahoga River and names it "Cleaveland."

1797 Lorenzo Carter arrives in Cleaveland and becomes the town's first nonnative resident.

1799 Nathaniel Doan constructs a hotel and tavern on one corner of Euclid Avenue and East 107th Street and a store on another. The area will be known as Doan's Corners.

1803 Ohio becomes the 17th state in the Union.

Woodcut of a boat ride on the Erie Canal in the 1820s.

1825 Construction of the Ohio & Erie Canal begins. Two years later, the canal's first segment, from Cleaveland to Akron, will open.

1831 The *Cleveland Advertiser* officially changes the spelling of the town's name when it drops the "a" in its title.

1845 John Baldwin forms the Baldwin Institute, one of Ohio's first colleges to accept all students regardless of gender or race, in Berea. The school will later be known as Baldwin-Wallace College.

1851 The Cleveland, Columbus, and Cincinnati Railroad begins service.

1870 John D. Rockefeller establishes the Standard Oil Company in Cleveland.

1870 Henry Sherwin and Edward Williams create the paint manufacturing company Sherwin, Williams & Company in Cleveland.

1876 Bedford native Archibald Willard paints the commemorative *Spirit of '76,* which hangs in the window of J. F. Ryder's photo studio in Cleveland until its unveiling in Philadelphia at the Centennial Exhibition of 1876.

1876 Euclid native Charles F. Brush creates his first electric dynamo, making way for his invention of the arc lamp.

1808 The Ohio General Assembly establishes Cuyahoga County. Two years later Cleaveland will be chosen as the county seat.

1818 *Walk-in-the-Water* becomes the first steamboat to sail on Lake Erie. The boat facilitates travel and trade between Cleaveland and other towns along the lake.

1818 The *Cleaveland Gazette & Commercial Register,* the town's first newspaper, is published.

1831 James A. Garfield is born in Orange Township. He will become the 20th president of the United States.

1836 Cleveland is incorporated as a city.

1842 The *Plain Dealer* newspaper publishes its first issue in Cleveland.

1845 The City Bank of Cleveland is founded. It will later be renamed the National City Bank.

1863 Postal worker Joseph Briggs of Cleveland persuades the Post Office to deliver mail to Cleveland residents' homes for free.

1869 The Lake View Cemetery is founded in Cleveland. Its residents will include James Garfield and John D. Rockefeller.

1869 John W. Heisman, inventor of the forward pass, is born in Cleveland. The coach's name will be immortalized in the Heisman Trophy college football award.

1881 U.S. president James Garfield is assassinated.

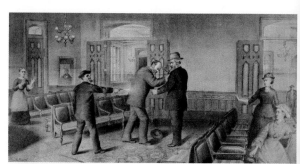

Assassination of President James A. Garfield, ca. 1881.

1882　1896　1905　1915

1882 Jeptha H. Wade grants 73 acres of land and 14 deer to Cleveland. The city uses the land to build Wade Park, the new site for the zoo.

1886 St. Ignatius College is established in Cleveland. In the 20th century it will be renamed John Carroll University and moved to University Heights.

1890 The Arcade, one of the nation's first indoor shopping centers, is founded in Cleveland.

1896 Alexander Winton creates an early version of the automobile in Cleveland. A year later he founds the Winton Motor Carriage Co. to manufacture Winton cars.

1900 The National Electric Lamp Association (NELA) is established in Cleveland. In 1911 it will be absorbed into General Electric and moved to Cleveland's newly built Nela Park, where it becomes the center of GE's lighting business.

1905 Jacob Sapirstein borrows $50 and begins selling postcards to Cleveland stores. His business will become known as American Greetings, a leading manufacturer and retailer of greeting cards.

1906 Dr. George Washington Crile of Cleveland Heights performs the first successful human blood transfusion. He will later cofound the Cleveland Clinic.

1908 Eight-year-old Bob Hope moves from England to Cleveland with his family. He will grow up to become a beloved entertainer who traveled around the world entertaining U.S. troops.

1915 The Cleveland Play House, Ohio's first regional theater, is established.

1915 The American League baseball team Cleveland Naps (named for infielder Napoleon Lajoie) changes its name to the Cleveland Indians.

1917 The Cleveland Metropolitan Park District, the state's first park district, is founded. By the 21st century, it will comprise more than 20,000 acres of parkland.

1918 The Detroit-Superior High Level Bridge, the first fixed bridge of its kind in Cleveland, is constructed over the Cuyahoga River. It will later be renamed the Veterans' Memorial Bridge.

Colonial Arcade, Cleveland, ca. 1908.

1912 Almeda Adams founds the Cleveland Music School Settlement, which gives music lessons to children without regard for payment. The school will become one of the nation's largest community music schools.

1912 Clarence A. Crane, owner of the Queen Victoria Chocolate Company in Cleveland, invents Life Savers to compensate for the summer drop in chocolate candy sales.

Detroit-Superior Bridge, Cleveland, 1916.

1920 The Cleveland Indians win their first World Series, against the Brooklyn Robins (later the Dodgers), scoring the first triple play, grand slam, and home run by a pitcher in a World Series.

TIMELINE

1923

1923 Cleveland resident Garrett A. Morgan patents the first three-position traffic signal.

1925 Paul Newman is born in Shaker Heights. He will become an Academy Award–winning actor, as well as a director, race car driver, food-company entrepreneur, and philanthropist.

Cleveland Municipal Airport, 1937.

1925 The Cleveland Municipal Airport, precursor to the Cleveland Hopkins International Airport, opens. In 1930 it will begin operating the world's first radio-equipped air-traffic control tower.

1929 American Greetings revolutionizes greeting-card shopping with the first self-service displays.

1930

1930 George Steinbrenner is born in Rocky River. He will become owner of Major League Baseball's New York Yankees, Iwhich won seven world championships during the tumultuous Steinbrenner era.

1930 Joe Shuster and Jerry Siegel meet for the first time at Glenville High School in Cleveland. Within three years they will create the comic book hero Superman.

1931 The Cleveland Municipal Stadium opens. Its tenants will include the Cleveland Indians and the National Football League's Cleveland Rams and Cleveland Browns.

1931 Severance Hall, home of the Cleveland Orchestra, opens its doors.

1931 North Olmsted launches the state's first municipally owned bus line.

Cleveland Stadium, 1931.

1936

Jesse Owens, 1936 Olympic Games, Berlin.

1936 Jesse Owens, a Cleveland East Technical High School graduate, wins four gold medals in track and field at the Berlin Olympics.

1937

1937 Jack Green and Joseph Lewis cofound the Progressive Mutual Insurance Company (later known simply as Progressive) in Cleveland.

1938 The Lakewood Little Theatre moves into the former Lucier Movie Theater in Lakewood. The venue will be rebuilt as the the Beck Center for the Arts complex.

1946 The Cleveland Browns join the All-America Football Conference. Four years later they will join the National Football League and win the championship.

1946 Brothers Bob and Joe Switzer establish DayGlo Color Corporation, specializing in fluorescent paints and dyes, in Cleveland.

1947 Shortly after Jackie Robinson joins the Brooklyn Dodgers, Larry Doby signs with the Cleveland Indians, becoming the first black player in the American League.

1947 1970 1995 2010

1947 Dr. Claude S. Beck, surgeon at Western Reserve University School of Medicine in Cleveland, performs the first successful defibrillation of a human heart.

1951 Alan Freed is hired as a disc jockey for Cleveland's WJW radio station. He will later coin the phrase "rock 'n' roll."

1959 The 2,342-mile St. Lawrence Seaway opens, enabling large commercial ships on the Atlantic Ocean to reach the Port of Cleveland.

1963 Cuyahoga Community College, Ohio's first community college, opens in the Greater Cleveland area.

1970 The Cleveland Cavaliers become a member of the National Basketball Association.

1973 Established in 1840, Cleveland's West Side Market is designated a National Historic Landmark.

1974 The Greater Cleveland Regional Transit Authority is created, providing public transportation throughout the area.

1975 Frank Robinson is named manager of the Cleveland Indians, becoming the first black to manage in Major Leagues Baseball.

1976 Harvey Pekar debuts his comic book series, *American Splendor*, which becomes an underground hit.

Hikers in Cuyahoga Valley National Park.

1964 Cleveland State University is founded in downtown Cleveland.

1967 Dr. Rene Favaloro pioneers coronary bypass surgery at the Cleveland Clinic.

1967 Carl B. Stokes is elected mayor of Cleveland, becoming the first African American mayor of a major U.S. city.

1969 Euclid native George Sweigert patents the first modern wireless telephone.

1989 Cleveland-born comedian Arsenio Hall begins hosting his own late-night talk show on Fox-TV.

1994 Jacobs Field, later renamed Progressive Field, becomes the new home of the Cleveland Indians. In 2008 readers of *Sports Illustrated* will vote it the best ballpark in Major League Baseball.

1995 The Rock and Roll Hall of Fame honoring the legends of rock opens in Cleveland.

1995 *The Drew Carey Show*, a sitcom based in Carey's hometown of Cleveland, debuts on ABC-TV.

2000 Cuyahoga Valley Park, located between Akron and Cleveland, receives national park status from Congress.

2002 Bedford High School graduate Halle Berry wins an Oscar for her performance in *Monster's Ball*.

2005 Cleveland is named one of the most livable U.S. cities by London's Economist Intelligence Unit.

2010 Cleveland Clinic named best cardiac care hospital *by U.S. News & World Report* for 16th year.

2010 The 116-year-old Soldiers and Sailors Monument reopens following a $2 million restoration.

2010 The RTA's new Stephanie Tubbs Jones Transit Center becomes Cleveland's first downtown bus hub.

2011 Ground is broken for the new Cleveland Medical Mart & Convention Center, opening in 2013.

FUTURE PERFECT: CUYAHOGA COUNTY

PARTONE

This page: People gather at dusk at the fountain at Settlers Landing Park along the Cuyahoga River in the Flats District of downtown Cleveland, with the Main Avenue Bridge in the background. Opposite page: A couple samples *la dolce vita* in Cleveland's Little Italy.

Quality of Life

A CERTAIN SAVOIR FAIRE

Maybe it's the breeze off Lake Erie. Maybe it's the mechanical bridges on the Cuyahoga River, dramatically illuminated at night, lifting, swinging, rolling back on circular rockers, making way for freighters coming upriver from the Great Lakes to the steel mills that still operate today. Or perhaps it's being on a variety of "nation's best" lists, from universities and hospitals to sustainable living. For these and many other reasons, Cuyahoga County exudes an aura of confidence and optimism.

A brawny industrial history and enviable geographic location are just two of the distinguishing features of Cuyahoga County, the 485-square-mile entity that encompasses Cleveland (the county seat), along with the City of Solon and more than 50 suburban communities. Its 1.3 million residents make it the most populous county in the state, part of a five-county metro area that accounts for more than 54 percent of the northeastern Ohio workforce and represents nearly every ethnic culture in the world.

With a growth rate of more than 32 percent during the last decade of the 20th century, downtown Cleveland was ranked as one of America's "emerging down-towns" by the Brookings Institution in 2005. Fulfilling the vision articulated by architect/planner Daniel Burnham more than a century ago, more than $4 billion has been allotted to new development over the next few years. The centerpiece of the downtown revitalization is the new $425 million Cleveland Medical Mart & Convention Center (MMCC), scheduled to open in 2013.

CHAPTER**ONE**

Operated by Medical Mart Partners, Inc., MMCC will include 120,000 square feet of permanent showrooms for major medical manufacturers and service providers, as well as 300,000 square feet of exhibit space and 100,000 square feet of high-tech, flexible meeting rooms. Conveniently linked to University Circle by Health Line, a new transit corridor, MMCC will create a critical mass of innovation and commerce throughout the worldwide healthcare community.

Greater Cleveland remains a manufacturing champion—ninth in the nation in 2009—adapting cutting-edge concepts in automation, electronics, and information technology to deliver the goods on time and on budget. The region is also an educational powerhouse and a transportation hub, employing hundreds of thousands of people in these sectors. Even during the recession, education and health care employment in the county actually grew 3.4 percent in the 12 months ending July 2009, according to the Bureau of Labor Statistics. Add to

those advantages one of the busiest Great Lakes ports and a highly trained workforce that enjoys an affordable cost of living—15th lowest in the nation in 2009, according to the Council for Community and Economic Research—and the benefits of living and working in Cleveland become even more apparent.

Fourteen Fortune 500 companies are headquartered in Cuyahoga County. Eaton Corporation (power management systems), the Progressive Corporation (property and casualty insurance), and Parker Hannifin Corporation (motion and control technologies) are among the leaders, along with dozens of other high-profile companies. From American Greetings to Sherwin-Williams, Nacco Industries to Rockwell Automation, these household names are a testament to the county's business-friendly environment and diversified economy.

Another household name that still resonates today is John Glenn. The Glenn Research Center, renamed for the former astronaut and Ohio senator in 1999, conducts research, development, and testing of new technologies and equipment to support NASA spaceflight missions and advance exploration of the solar system.

This page: The Great Lakes Science Center is among Cleveland's many cultural attractions. Opposite page, from left: Visitors explore the tropical foliage at the Cleveland Botanical Garden in University Circle; a young Cleveland Indians fan raises a glove in front of the statue of pitching great Bob Feller.

Cuyahoga County's financial health is strong, as evidenced by its AA+ bond rating from Standard & Poor's in 2009. The county seat is a well-established financial center, home base for the Federal Reserve Bank of Cleveland, serving Ohio, western Pennsylvania, eastern Kentucky, and the northern West Virginia panhandle. Nearly 30 financial institutions, including Fortune 500 companies KeyCorp, PNC Financial Services Group, and Fifth Third Bank of Northeastern Ohio, along with the regional Dollar Bank, operate branches in the area. The county is an inviting place for insurance companies such as Progressive, Medical Mutual of Ohio, and the innovative Insurance.com.

In addition, nine Ohio-based venture capital funds ensure a steady flow of new products and technologies, particularly in the fields of health and life sciences. Among them are state-sponsored Ohio Third Frontier and county-sponsored New Product Development and Entrepreneurship Loan Fund. County resources such as research and development loans, revenue bonds, and grants provide added incentives for entrepreneurs to generate ideas and start new businesses.

An excellent infrastructure, effective management, and a strong economy are only part of what makes this midwestern metropolis on Lake Erie so appealing. There is a museum dedicated exclusively to rock 'n' roll. A vibrant arts scene (nurtured by the Cleveland-based Cuyahoga Arts and Culture, one

of the largest publicly supported arts funding organizations in the nation). Excellent universities. One of the country's best science centers. Beautiful nature preserves and parks. Even sports fans find a haven here.

From their relatively new stadium (1999) at North Coast Harbor, the Cleveland Browns carry on an NFL tradition that dates back to 1946, fielding Jim Brown, Ozzie Newsome, and other Hall of Famers over the years. The Cleveland Indians, part of baseball's American League since 1901 (Cy Young started here in 1890 with the Cleveland Spiders), play ball at Progressive Field (formerly Jacobs Field), built in 1994 as part of the Gateway Sports and Entertainment Complex. Although superstar LeBron James is no longer in the lineup, the Cleveland Cavaliers play their NBA home games at Quicken Loans Arena, also part of the Gateway complex.

Superstars of rock 'n' roll, a term coined by Cleveland disc jockey Alan Freed, are honored at the Rock and Roll Hall of Fame and Museum. Designed by renowned architect I. M. Pei and rising above the Lake Erie shoreline near Browns Stadium, the museum has provided a fitting home for the sights, sounds, and legends of rock 'n' roll since its opening in 1995.

In 1918, long before the legends of rock were even born, the Cleveland Orchestra began perfecting its sound. One of the world's most sought-after ensembles, the orchestra plays in its landmark home, Severance Hall (considered one of the most beautiful concert halls on the planet) and in venues around the globe.

Of course, rock, jazz, blues, funk, punk, and metal bands perform in the innumerable clubs and concert venues that have sprung up around Greater Cleveland, especially in the historic downtown Warehouse District.

The second decade of the 20th century was a watershed for local theater. In 1915, Cleveland witnessed two bold American firsts: the opening of a professional theater company, the Cleveland Play House; and a neighborhood settlement house devoted to interracial theater that evolved into Karamu House, a magnet for top African American talent. Both theaters have staged productions with some of the biggest names in the business, from Hal Holbrook and Tom Hanks to Langston Hughes and Ruby Dee.

Opposite page, from left: The play's the thing at the Cleveland Play House; The Boss greets visitors to the Rock and Roll Hall of Fame.
This page: Patrons sample the wares at a nightclub in Cleveland's Warehouse District.

These venues are joined by stages all across the county. Playhouse Square, Cuyahoga County's nationally renowned theater district on Euclid Avenue, is the second-largest such district in the nation, after New York's. Its five play-houses were built in the 1920s and restored in the 1970s–80s. The renova-tions lured new business to the neighborhood, and today the district is alive with retail, restaurants, and chic apartments and lofts. Adding to the county's full compliment of performing arts are the Cleveland Public Theatre, the region's leading stage for experimental plays, and the Chagrin Valley Little Theatre, one of the nation's oldest community theaters.

More than 40 cultural, educational, and medical institutions are found among the parklike 500 acres of University Circle. The Cleveland Museum of Art exhibits 46,000 works that span every country and era. A significant renovation, scheduled for completion in 2012, will expand the museum's space by 199,000

This page, from left: Playhouse Square is the heart of Cleveland Theater District; visitors form a favorable impression of this work at the Cleveland Museum of Art. Opposite page: Severance Hall is home to the venerated Cleveland Orchestra.

square feet, including the addition of a glass-covered courtyard, and completely restore a 1916 beaux arts structure and a 1971 masterpiece designed by Marcel Breuer. The Museum of Contemporary Art Cleveland will take up residence in a new, nearly 34,000-square-foot space in University Circle in 2012. MOCA interprets culture through the works of both internationally renowned and emerging or established northeastern Ohio contemporary artists.

MOCA's new location in University Circle will put it front and center of a $300 million mixed-use project called Uptown, the University Arts and Retail District. Powered by Case Western Reserve University (CWRU), the development along Euclid Avenue and on part of the CWRU campus will restore the district's historic aspects and transform it into a sought-after visitor destination.

A vitally important district for Clevelanders, University Circle also contains the Cleveland Institute of Art, one of the top 10 U.S. colleges of art and design, and the Cleveland Institute of Music, among the nation's leading conservatories. It's also the location of the Cleveland Orchestra's Severance Hall, the 10-acre Cleveland Botanical Garden, and the Cleveland Museum of Natural History.

In addition to a plethora of museums, shops, hotels, and restaurants (Little Italy is here as well), the district is home to the Cleveland Clinic and University Hospitals Case Medical Center, two of the nation's most highly regarded hospital systems. They're joined in the Circle by at least 15 other organizations devoted to health, from the American Cancer Society and Bioenterprise Corporation to the Hitchcock Center for Women.

Residents can pursue a healthful lifestyle at Cleveland MetroParks, an "Emerald Necklace" of 16 nature preserves that encircle the city with trails, fishing holes, and golf courses. Cuyahoga Valley National Park's 33,000 acres follow the Cuyahoga ("crooked" in the Algonquian language) River as it winds through forests and waterfalls, ravines and farmland between Cleveland and Akron. The 20-mile Ohio & Erie Canal Towpath Trail follows the historic canal route through the park. Lake Erie's sandy beaches paint a creamy swath of tan across northern Cuyahoga County. The City of Solon's new Veterans Memorial Park, which opened in May 2010, features a lit fountain surrounded by monuments and flags for each of the seven branches of the military.

Endowed with natural beauty, a haven for arts and education, a business powerhouse, and a leader in health care, Cuyahoga County has a dazzling future.

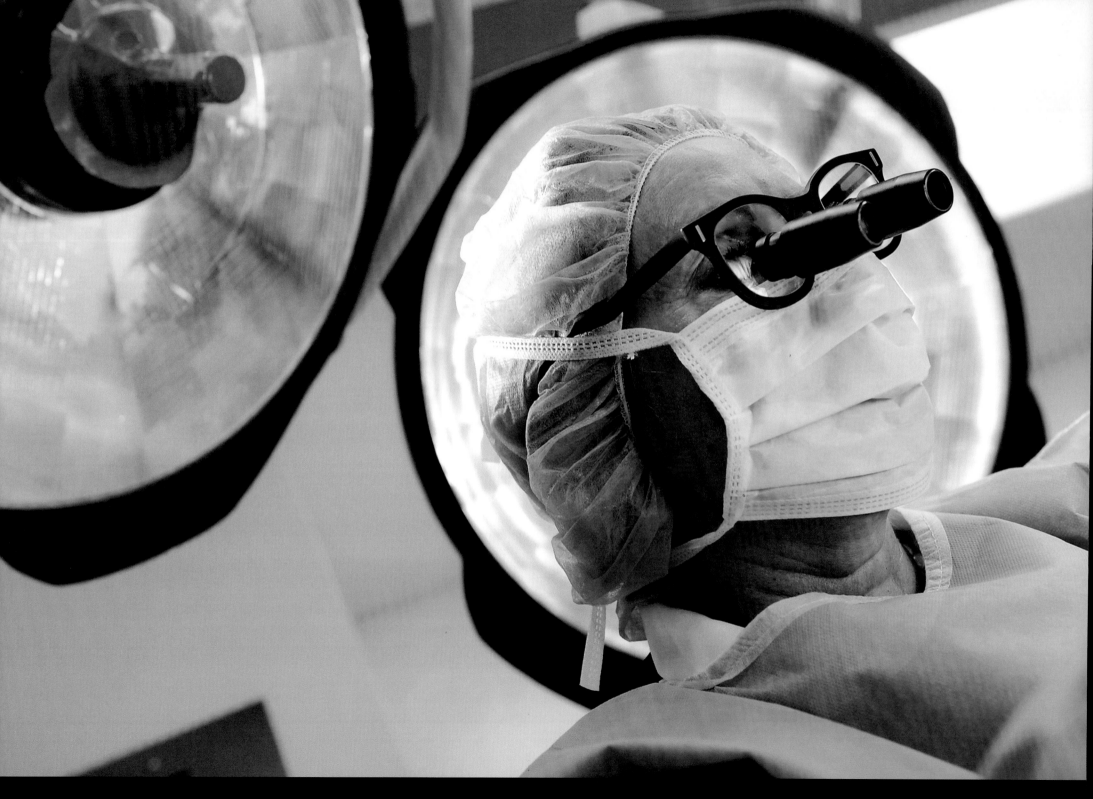

This page: Doctors at the Cleveland Clinic were the first to perform a face transplant. Opposite page: The exterior of University Hospitals, one of the region's

CHAPTER TWO

Innovations in Health Care
and Biotechnology

THE VITALITY SECTOR

Cuyahoga County is emerging as a global leader in innovative health care and biotechnology. Located along the Cleveland Health-Tech Corridor on Euclid Avenue is a world-class health care and research system, including the Cleveland Clinic, University Hospitals Case Medical Center, and more than 100 biomedical and technology companies. Conducting vital research and developing innovative approaches to patient care, Greater Cleveland-area health care centers have earned national recognition for excellence in a variety of specialties, from neonatal care to cardiovascular.

Health care and biotechnology are vital to the growth of the region's economy. In 2009 the health care sector employed 13 percent of the Cuyahoga County workforce, second only to manufacturing, the traditional employment leader, at 16 percent. The new Cleveland Medical Mart & Convention Center, scheduled to open in 2013, will host as many as 80 medical conventions and meetings per year, further boosting the region's economy.

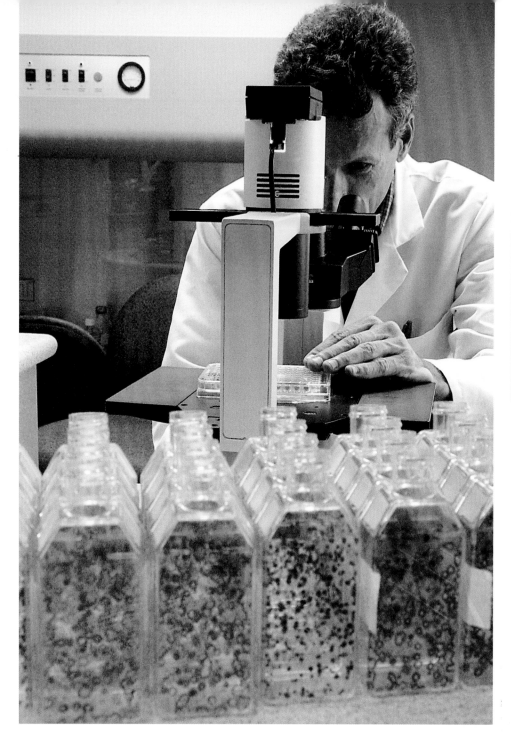

Health Care Systems

Cleveland area health care systems enjoy a well-deserved reputation for providing quality medical care for area residents. The Cleveland Clinic, which opened in 1921, is one of the nation's largest health care centers, with a main campus in Cleveland and affiliate hospitals throughout the country. In 2009 the Sydell and Arnold Miller Family Heart & Vascular Institute was ranked #1 in America by *U.S. News & World Report* for the 15th consecutive year, and the Children's Hospital was ranked #4 in the nation for neurology and neurosurgery. The Lerner Research Institute, home to the Cleveland Clinic's biomedical research, is at the forefront of cancer research, developing a promising prototype vaccine to prevent breast cancer. Doctors come from around the world for residency training and advance fellowships at the Education Institute.

University Hospitals Case Medical Center, a 1,032-bed medical center and tertiary-care hospital, has been recognized as one of the top 50 hospitals in six medical and surgical specialties. Its individual centers include the Ireland Cancer Center, one of the top Comprehensive Cancer Centers in the United States and only one of 12 facilities with a drug pipeline for early-phase clinical

trials. In 2010 20 percent of the patients were enrolled in these studies, as opposed to 4 percent at other facilities. The Rainbow Babies & Children's Hospital was ranked #4 in the nation for neonatal care by *U.S. New & World Report* in 2009 and #1 in neonatal congenital hearth surgery by the Society of Thoracic Surgery. The MacDonald Women's Hospital, which has served women in the Buckeye State for more than 100 years, is the only facility in Ohio devoted exclusively to female health care.

People are the backbone of any effective health care system, and the doctors and nurses at the MetroHealth System are among the best in the nation. All of MetroHealth's active staff physicians are on the faculty of Case Western Reserve University School of Medicine, an affiliate since 1914, and a sizable number were ranked among the Best Doctors in America in 2009–2010. In 2010 MetroHealth was among the elite group of hospitals to be granted the Magnet Recognition Program Re-designation, the nation's highest honor for excellence in nursing care. MetroHealth's level-one trauma center has a state-of-the-art Critical Care Pavilion that includes a Trauma Center, Comprehensive Burn Care Center, and Surgical Intensive Care Units. The MetroHealth Rehabilitation Institute of Ohio, the largest hospital-based rehabilitation program in Ohio, is one of only 14 rehabilitation facilities in the nation designated by the National Institute on Disability and Rehabilitation Research as a Model System program for the rehabilitation of patients with spinal cord injuries.

Providing care and healing for the afflicted has been the mission of St. Vincent Charity Medical Center (formerly St. Vincent Charity Hospital) since 1865. Located in downtown Cleveland's campus district, the 485-bed facility provides patients with access to full range of medical and surgical specialties, including 24-hour emergency care. In 2010 HealthGrades ranked St. Vincent in the top 5 percent for its clinical quality, placing it among HealthGrade's Distinguished

Hospitals for Clinical Excellence. St. Vincent has also enjoyed five-star ratings from HealthGrades for its treatment of heart failure for eight consecutive years, beginning in 2003, and the Spine and Orthopedic Institute is ranked as one of Ohio's top five spine surgery facilities. Affiliated with the Harvard Medical School facility, the Joslin Diabetes Center is a leader in the treatment of adults with Type 1 and Type 2 diabetes, using a collaborative, multidisciplinary approach in applying the latest research and treatment advances.

Innovations in Biotechnology

Biotechnology initiatives have helped to revitalize the health care sector and pump new lifeblood into the Greater Cleveland economy. Biotech, an initiative designed to stimulate growth and development of biomedical companies, has helped create or accelerate the growth of more than 80 companies and attract more than $925 million in new funding. Biotech's founders and partners include such health care and research powerhouses as Case Western Reserve University, the Cleveland Clinic, and University Hospitals Case Medical Center. Using such criteria as research and development funding, investment, and biotech patents, *Business Facilities* ranked Biotech #4 in the nation for bioscience business in 2009.

Opposite page, from left: Antibodies are produced at the LRI Hybridoma Core at the Cleveland Clinic; University Hospitals reside on the campus of Case Western University. This page:The MetroHealth System's Critical Care Pavilion opened in Cleveland in 2004.

Taking ideas generated in the university's laboratories and classrooms and turning them into viable commercial ventures is the mission of the Case Western University Technology Transfer Center. Inventions are carefully evaluated as to their commercial merit; of 100 inventions submitted to the center, as few as 30 may eventually be submitted for patents.

Cleveland Clinic Innovation helps to realize the innovative potential of the Cleveland Clinic, commercializing the inventions generated by the clinic. Using a comprehensive approach, it creates spin-off companies, secures licenses, and establishes strategic collaborations with corporate partners. Its success is demonstrated in the more than 200 new inventions per year and 24 companies that have been spun off since 2000.

Led by the Cleveland Clinic, the Global Cardiovascular Innovation Center (GCIC) is a consortium of nearly 20 academic, medical, government, and industry partners devoted to cardiovascular research and product development. Founded in 2007 with a $60 million grant from the state's Third Frontier Project, GCIC facilitates the development and adoption of new diagnostic tools, pharmaceuticals, and medical devices for cardiovascular diseases. Among the companies under the GCIC umbrella is the Atrial Fibrillation Innovation Center, where a team of leading researchers and clinicians is exploring new diagnostic and therapeutic approaches for treating atrial fibrillation, a common, debilitating heart rhythm condition. Cleveland HeartLab is developing molecular biomarker technologies and diagnostic tests focused on managing and reducing inflammation, a major cause of heart disease. Athersys is using potent adult progenitor cells to create a pharmaceutical technology for the treatment of congestive heart failure. Using a set of tissue-specific peptides, Cell Targeting is developing a drug delivery platform that ultimately can be used to deliver cellular therapies to the diseased heart.

From lab to bedside marks the approach of University Hospitals' Center for Clinical Research, the largest biomedical research center in Ohio and one of top 15 in the country. The center's team of investigators uses translational research—the clinical application of scientific medical research—to achieve breakthroughs in the treatment of life-threatening diseases. Discoveries have helped in the early detection of cancer and other serious illnesses, higher survival rates for metastatic cancer patients, improved outcomes in organ transplants, better care for premature babies, and minimally invasive procedures for joint replacement.

A half-century after John Glenn became the first American to orbit the earth, space exploration is generating new technologies that are applicable for health care on earth. NASA's Glenn Research Center has pioneered a new biomedical sensor called Biomedical Microelectromechanical Systems, or Bio-MEMS.

This page: A trainer gives some pointers to a woman during a spinning class. Opposite page: A Zero Locomotion Simulator is tested out at the Glenn Research Center, part of a weightlessness study conducted by the Cleveland Clinic for NASA in 2008.

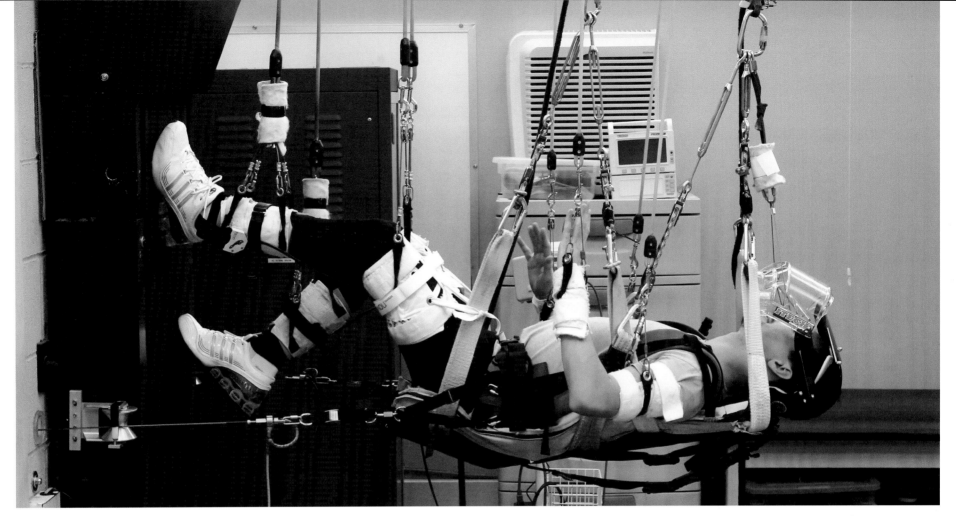

Made of gold and silicon, the sensors are about the size of the head of a pin—1 millimeter wide and .5 millimeters thick. Each tiny sensor also includes a multi-turn loop antenna, allowing data to be wirelessly transmitted from the sensor to an external unit. Glenn signed an agreement with Entronix, a company that is using the technology to develop a device for measuring blood pressure and heart rate that could benefit millions of people. The absence of a wire reduces the risk of infection, and the user-friendly external readers allow patients to take their own readings. The technology may have applications for other areas, such as general surgery and bone, neck, and spine health.

The John Glenn Biomedical Engineering Consortium (JGBEC) brings together the medical expertise and research capabilities of the Glenn Research Center, Case Western Reserve University (CWRU), Cleveland Clinic, University Hospitals of Cleveland (UHC), and the National Center for Space Exploration Research (NCSER). The consortium's mission is to apply technologies to reduce health risks for astronauts and the general population. From dynamic light-scattering technology came Space Goggles, a head-mounted device resembling night-vision goggles that can be used to diagnose and monitor diseases of the eye such as cataracts, as well as serious conditions as diabetes and Alzheimer's.

From the far reaches of outer space to the inner workings of the region's research labs and hospitals, the prognosis for Greater Cleveland's health care and biotechnology industries is robust.

COLORACCENTS
INTERIOR LATEX
Satin

SHERWIN WILLIAMS

ULTRADEEP BASE
MUST BE TINTED BEFORE USING
Y38 T 154
6403-49668

590 fl oz
(4³⁹⁄₆₄) U.S. Gal

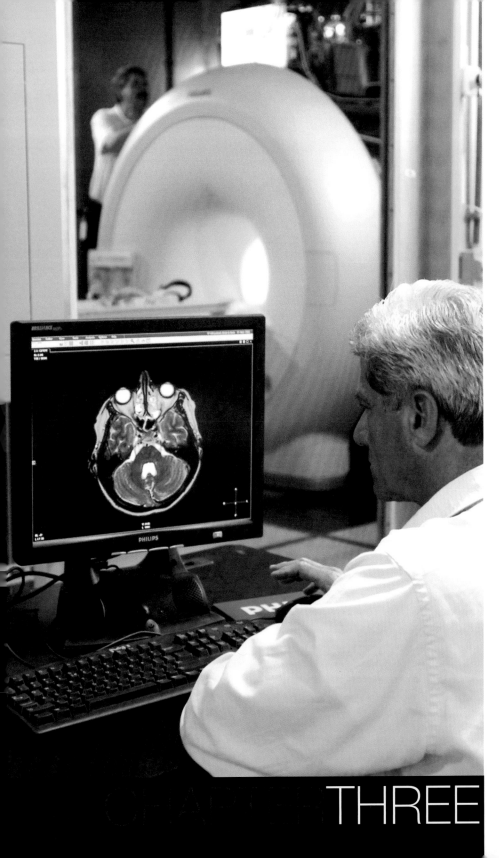

THREE

MADE IN CUYAHOGA COUNTY

What steel and automobiles were to the Cuyahoga County economy in the second half of the twentieth century, the MRI and defibrillator are to the Greater Cleveland economy of the twenty-first century. With more than $800 million in investment since 2003 and a highly skilled workforce, the region supports more than 600 biomedical businesses. While the nation was still reeling from a severe recession in 2010, Greater Cleveland's biomedical device industry was enjoying a 34 percent growth over five years.

Beginning in 2013, major medical manufacturers and service providers will be able to exhibit their wares in the new Cleveland Medical Mart & Convention Center. Located in downtown Cleveland, this $425 million state-of-the-art facility will house 120,000 square feet of permanent exhibit space for cardiology, surgery, OB/GYN, orthopedics, imaging, medical devices, and more, providing an integrated market center for clinicians, suppliers, purchasers, service providers, and others in the medical and health care industries.

Stimulated by research coming out of area universities, biomedical businesses are making significant advances in MRI-based technology. A leader in the medical imaging industry, Philips Healthcare has introduced such innovations as the Allura Xper, an interventional X-ray system designed to visualize vessel structure beyond a clot to help physicians assess the size and extent of a stroke. Other Philips innovations include Heart-Start, an automated home defibrillator, and the Achieva, a 7.OT MRI whole body scanner installed at the Cleveland facility's MRI research center.

Located in Oakwood Village, ViewRay has developed the Renaissance System. Designed for use in radiation treatment, it sends dynamic images of the position of the tumor, allowing for more precise targeting of the growth with the radiation dose. Interventional Imaging, Inc. (I^{3}MRI), formed in collaboration with Case Western Reserve University, employs technologies developed at the University Hospitals of Cleveland. I^{3}MRI has developed a disposable catheter that contains micro-coils and electronics for communicating with MRI scanners.

Diagnosing heart disease, the leading cause of death in the United States, has reached new levels of precision with CardioInsight's Electrocardiographic Mapping (ECM), which combines body surface electrical data with heart-torso anatomical data to provide 3-D images of electrical activity for the entire heart. A disposable multi-sensor body surface array and hardware capture surface data, and sophisticated software computes and visualizes epicardial 3-D electronatoic maps and electrograms of the whole heart.

People with spinal injuries and other orthopedic conditions can look to innovations from companies such as AxioMed Spine Corporation, which has developed the next generation of artificial discs. The Freedom Lumbar Disc uses a patented polymer that, in combination with the implant design, provides three-dimensional motion that works in harmony with the natural biomechanics of the spine. Designed to withstand the wear that occurs over decades of use, the viscoelastic disc was being tested in clinical trials in 2010, and, if approved, will provide relief for younger lumbar patients.

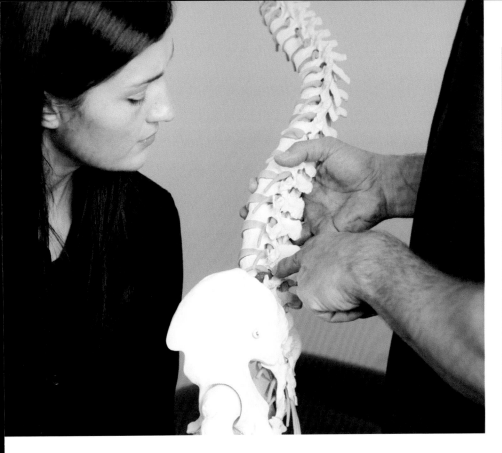

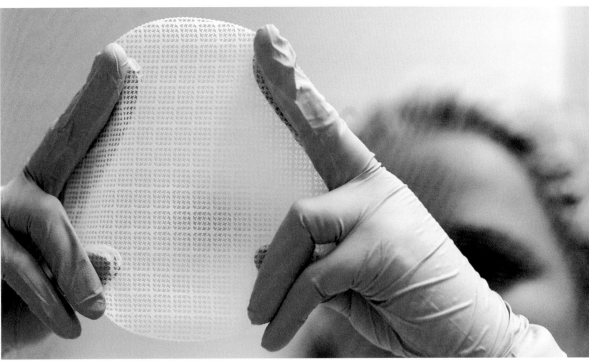

Merlot OrthopediX may sound like the latest vintage from the Napa Valley. In fact, the Cleveland-area medical technology company has produced a groundbreaking solution for bone anchorage—a patent-protected open helix bone screw. This implant technology has spine, trauma, and general orthopedic applications.

For the millions of people who suffer from sleep and movement disorders, relief may be on the way. Cleveland Medical Devices is pioneering sophisticated technologies to diagnose and treat sleep disorders and to restore control and function to patients with a variety of neurological disorders such as Parkinson's disease and cerebral palsy. The wireless Kinesia HomeView, an ambulatory motor assessment system, uses Crystal PSG software, a user-friendly software package for data acquisition, scoring, and reporting at home.

The Greater Cleveland area is at the forefront of newly emergent neurostimulation technologies. Neuros Medical's Nerve Block, an electrode powered by a pacemaker-sized generator, delivers high-frequency stimulation to sensory nerves in the peripheral nervous system to block chronic limb pain, postsurgical pain, and migraine. Partnering with strategic investors, venture capital firms, and angel networks, NDI Medical is an incubator for developing innovative neurostimulation technologies. Intelect Medical is focused on advancing deep brain stimulation (DBS) therapy for improving the recovery of chronic stroke and traumatic brain injury patients. Synapse Biomedical's NeuRx Diaphragm Pacing System is a minimally invasive outpatient procedure that establishes a deeper and more comfortable breathing pattern for spinal cord injury patients, thus reducing their dependency on mechanical ventilation.

Among the biomedical companies establishing new facilities in the Cleveland area is Proxy Biomedical. Headquartered in Ireland, the company invested $1.5 million in capital in its U.S. headquarters, which serves as a market development site for new product platforms. This full-service operation develops and manufactures biomaterials for the repair and regeneration of tissue for advanced surgical procedures. The MotifMESH MacroPorous NW Implant is universal surgical implant suitable for different types of fascial defects, including ventral hernia repair.

Opposite page: To sleep, perhance to dream . . . this is the hope of sleep-study subjects. This page, from left: A student examines a model of a spine; MOTIFMesh, a tissue-engineering biomaterial created by Proxy Biomedical, is used in tissue regeneration.

27

With annual sales exceeding $15 billion, Eaton Corporation, a global technology leader in electrical components and systems, makes its corporate headquarters in Cleveland. Eaton produces systems and components to help the aerospace, automotive, truck, electrical, and hydraulic industries use power more efficiently. Its clients such industry powerhouses as Airbus, Caterpillar, Shell, and Volkswagen. Also headquartered in Cleveland, Parker Hannifin is the world's leading diversified manufacturer of motion and control technologies and systems, providing precision-engineered solutions for a wide variety of mobile, industrial, and aerospace companies.

Several companies play a vital supporting role in the Cleveland area's biotech industry. Sea Air Space Machining & Molding machine-tools metal and plastic parts for medical businesses such as Philips HealthCare. Cleveland Vibrator's tiny turbine vibrators are used by the makers of pharmaceuticals and dental products. Sparton Medical Systems provides a full range of contract services from design to manufacturing, delivering specialized solutions for fluid handling, laser technology, and electronic modules and sensor systems.

The Energizer Bunny, which celebrated its 20th anniversary in 2009, promotes the diverse array of batteries produced by Energizer Holdings, Inc., a global leader in batteries and personal care products. Subsidiaries Schick-Wilkinson Sword and Playtex produce everything from wet shave products to Playtex gloves. The company conducts research and development at the Energizer Global Technology Center in Westlake.

Advanced Manufacturing

Having mastered the ABC's of heavy industry, the Greater Cleveland area has graduated to advanced manufacturing—the application of cutting-edge concepts in electronics, computers, software, and automation to improve production. More than 6,000 manufacturing firms, including more than a dozen Fortune 500 firms, are headquartered in the Greater Cleveland area. Producing a diverse array of produces and services, from plastics and chemicals to metalworking and industrial machinery, these companies account for 16 percent of employment and 20 percent of gross output in northeast Ohio. They have ready access to innovative research and technologies from the more than 300 industrial research laboratories that make their home here.

The transmission of energy on a larger scale is facilitated by Performed Line Products, a Mayfield Heights company that designs and manufacturers cable anchoring hardware and systems, high-speed cross-connect devices, and more for energy, communications, and other businesses. Rockwell Automation provides industrial automation control and information solutions, from stand-alone, industrial components to enterprise-wide integrated systems.

The Cleveland area paints with bold strokes in the production of plastics, polymers, and chemicals. A worldwide brand for paints and pigments, Sherwin–Williams produces a diverse array of products, including chemicals, soaps and cleaners, rubber products, clay and concrete products, and adhesives and sealants. Innovative approaches to polymers are coming out of the

This page: Like the Energizer Bunny, Lew Urr, who developed the first commercially viable alkaline battery, is still going strong. Opposite page, from left: An assembly line worker at Ford's Cleveland Engine Plant No. 1; the Applied Industrial Technologies headquarters in Cleveland's Midtown Corridor.

labs at the University of Akron's College of Polymer Science and Polymer Engineering and Case Western Reserve University's Macromolecular Institute.

The impressive list of manufacturing companies in the Cleveland area also includes Aleris International (primary metals); Applied Industrial Technologies; Ferro (colorants); Lincoln Electric Holdings (welding/cutting products); Nacco Industries (housewares and material handling); OM Group (metal-based specialty chemicals); and Swagelok (fluid system valves, fittings, pumps, tubing, and accessories).

The rejuvenative powers of Cleveland's manufacturing sector is no more aptly illustrated than by the case of Ford Motor Company's Cleveland Engine Plant No. 1. Closed down in 2007, the historic plant reopened in 2009 to begin pre-production of fuel-efficient, high-performance EcoBoost V-6 engines. Ford's Cleveland Casting Plant is also in full production, making cast iron engine blocks and engine components for Ford plants throughout North America.

Manufacturing in Greater Cleveland is not limited to industrial products. American Greetings, based in Cleveland, is the #2 producer of greeting cards in the United States. L'Oreal, the global hair care and cosmetics giant, maintains a manufacturing plant and consumer evaluation center in Solon.

Cleveland is also home to the Northeast Ohio's largest distributor of food service products and restaurant supplies. Sysco Cleveland, Inc. distributes fresh and frozen meat, poultry, seafood, fruits and vegetables, canned and dry products, paper and disposable products, cleaning supplies, and kitchen equipment to restaurants, hotels, schools, hospitals, and other customers in the Greater Cleveland area.

Transforming the region's manufacturing economy into a global player is essential to continued economic development. Start-up companies and established businesses can turn to MAGNET, the Manufacturing Advocacy & Growth Network. Its broad range of services includes product design and development, improvement in the efficiency and productivity of manufacturing processes, integrated approaches to becoming sustainable, and employee training. In 2009 alone, MAGNET's services led to cost savings of more than $25 million and generated more than $33 million in investment—a promising sign that this vital sector of the Greater Cleveland economy is embracing new ideas and positioning itself for continued growth and development.

This page: Renowned architect Frank Gehry designed the Weatherhead School of Management for Case Western Reserve University in Cleveland.

Opposite page: Striking Gothic architecture is found on the campus of John Carroll University.

Higher Education

SMART START ON SUCCESS

Acquiring an education is one of the smartest things a person can do. And acquiring it in Cuyahoga County brings an added dimension—that of learning in one of the nation's most vibrant metropolises. Founders of at least half a dozen colleges and universities spotted the area's potential back in the 19th century. Today there are more than 15 institutions of higher learning in Cuyahoga County alone, and most of them appear on lists of the nation's best colleges. Whether public or private, large or small, educational institutions in the area draw upon a tradition of excellence and a vision for the future.

Cleveland State University (CSU), a public university founded in 1964, has the largest enrollment of the county's four-year schools—16,418 students in 2009. That's more than a 4 percent increase over the year before, and a whopping 47.5 percent increase in new graduate students. In part because the economic downturn is driving students back to universities across the nation, this increase is also due to CSU's reputation for great programs in business, biomedical research, education, and law. To accommodate this growth, CSU is in the midst of a $250 million makeover that is transforming its 85-acre downtown Cleveland campus into an inviting residential setting. (Two extension campuses, in Westlake and Solon, enable those in the suburbs to take classes closer to home.) CSU also offers Division I sports, in the form of the Cleveland State Vikings, and the school has been tapped to host the NCAA Men's Basketball Tournament at Quicken Loans Arena in 2011.

CHAPTERFOUR

research universities in the nation and has nearly 100 interdisciplinary research centers. An annual endowment of about $1.4 billion, coupled with roughly $375 million in external awards, enables the school to affect virtually everything that goes on in the state and nation, from medicine to sustainability. It's no wonder that more than half (57 percent) of the 9,738 students enrolled in 2009 were graduate and professional students.

As the new decade unfolds, Case Western is focusing on interdisciplinary alliances in four areas that will define society's future: energy and the environment; human health; culture, creativity, and design; and social justice and ethics. Driving the environmental focus are several CWRU centers, including the innovative Great Lakes Energy Institute, which explores leading-edge energy alternatives such as freshwater wind power, and the Center for Business as an Agent of World Benefit, which advances understanding throughout the world of the link between the environment and quality of life.

With eight colleges (from liberal arts to law), 33 research institutes, and 200 undergraduate majors, CSU is a magnet for partnerships with corporations and organizations in the area. The CSU Maxine Goodman Levin College of Urban Affairs—one of the nation's top schools for urban affairs and the only one in Ohio—leads a group of eight research universities in the Ohio Urban University Program. Studies from the group have an impact on state policy on issues ranging from business tax reform to land redevelopment and contribute to research at several federal centers.

Research is also the hallmark of Cleveland's Case Western Reserve University (CWRU), the first college to open in northern Ohio, in 1826. Then called Western Reserve College and situated in nearby Hudson, it was moved to its present location in 1882. Case Western ranks among the top 25 private

In the realm of human health, the CWRU School of Medicine and its teaching hospital, the University Hospitals Case Medical Center, constitute the largest biomedical research center in Ohio. In 2002 the university and one of the area's top health systems together established the CWRU Cleveland Clinic Lerner College of Medicine, which mentors students to become physician-scientists specializing in biomedical research. On the cultural front, alliances incorporating art, architecture, music, theater, and literature are exploring the interactions of culture, creativity, and design on one another. To advance social justice, the avant-garde Inamori International Center for Ethics and Excellence investigates the common thread of humanity in cultures around the world as it fosters ethical leadership.

At the other end of the collegiate spectrum from large, internationally renowned universities are small liberal arts colleges, where the student-faculty

Established in 1845 and affiliated with the United Methodist Church, the school enrolls 4,300 in its graduate and undergraduate programs and is highly regarded for its Bach institute, conservatory, and offerings in musical theater as well as neuroscience. Ursuline College, a women-focused Catholic college established in 1871 in Pepper Pike, draws about 1,400 students (both men and women) to its graduate and undergraduate schools and offers a sought-after graduate program in art therapy and counseling.

ratio dips into the teens and attention focuses on the individual. The most acclaimed of Cuyahoga County's smaller four-year schools is John Carroll University (JCU), a Jesuit school long considered one of the top 10 colleges in the Midwest. Situated in University Heights, JCU was another early entry on Ohio's educational map, founded in 1886 as St. Ignatius College. Today JCU enrolls 3,800 students, both graduate and undergraduate, in its College of Arts and Sciences and John M. and Mary Jo Boler School of Business. The latter earned accreditation in both business and accounting from the Association to Advance Collegiate Schools of Business (AACSB) International—an honor earned by only 11 percent of the world's business schools. The university is fully coeducational, its centers and programs of study reflecting the Jesuit commitment to leadership and service. The Edward M. Muldoon Center for Entrepreneurship, for example, serves as a resource for entrepreneurs and their employees. The interdisciplinary Poverty and Solidarity course explores the causes and effects of poverty, with the goal of heightening students' motivation to help alleviate them. An interdisciplinary master's degree in nonprofit administration is geared to enabling students to respond to the region's socio-economic needs.

Several other small colleges in the area also top the list of leading midwestern liberal arts colleges, primary among them Baldwin–Wallace College in Berea.

Notre Dame College, a coeducational baccalaureate school in South Euclid, is known for programs in business, education, science—and athletics. After snagging an all-sports ranking of 34th nationally in the 2008–09 National Association of Intercollegiate Athletics (NAIA) Directors' Cup, the Notre Dame Falcons now compete in NCAA Division II athletics.

Clearly, Cuyahoga County is rich in high-quality campuses. But the selection doesn't end here—in fact, it's just begun. Those in the arts know that Cleveland has two internationally known professional colleges: the Cleveland Institute of Art (CIA) and the Cleveland Institute of Music (CIM). Situated in the city's cultural hub, University Circle, both institutions attract serious students determined to make a difference through their art, and both provide a full calendar of exhibits, films, and concerts for the community.

The older of the two schools, the Institute of Art, has been offering art classes of every sort since its founding in 1882 and bachelor of fine arts degrees since 1947. About 500 students enroll each year, choosing from 16 majors that are organized into creative "communities" for design, materials, visual arts and technologies, and integrated media. A perk not offered at many art schools is that students get their own studio space when they're ready to work on their

major. Others include the institute's galleries and lecture series, surpassed in popularity only by the alternative film series in the Cinematheque.

With a high-octane education under their belts, CIA graduates are frequently offered internships in companies throughout Ohio and the nation, including Fisher Price in New York, the Smithsonian Institution in Washington, and Walt Disney Imagineering in Glendale, California.

The Institute of Music, founded in 1920, ranks among the nation's top music conservatories; its alumni can be found in many of the world's leading orchestras and music companies. Renowned as a relatively small conservatory with a world-class faculty, the school engages 35 members of the Cleveland Orchestra as professors. About 450 students from around the world study in the bachelor's, master's, and doctoral degree programs, and

This page: This car design was produced by a GM intern from the Cleveland Institute of Art, whose work was featured on a Discovery Channel documentary.
Opposite page, from left: Exterior of the Cleveland Institute of Music; then-Senator Barack Obama addresses students at Cuyahoga Community College in 2007.

another 1,500, including children, take lessons at the institute. An affiliation with CWRU enables CIM degree candidates to take liberal arts classes at Case Western, while Case students balance the scales by taking music classes at the institute. Even with a less accomplished faculty, the institute would be tempting for its facilities and technology, including state-of-the-art recording studios and performance spaces and a comprehensive music library that is linked to the Case Western library.

By nature of their limited enrollments, small private colleges and professional institutes have to be selective, but increasingly, some of the larger schools are, as well. When accessibility and affordability are priorities, there are other options—and none beats the community colleges and career centers.

A leading public two-year college, Cuyahoga Community College (Tri-C) has campuses in downtown Cleveland, Parma, and Highland Hills, with a new Westshore campus that opened in January 2011. Ohio's first community

college (opened in 1963), it offers affordable tuition and more than 140 career, technical, and liberal arts programs to the 55,000 students who attend annually. The school also earns kudos for its science, engineering, and the health programs, along with its two-campus Corporate College for entre-preneur and workforce training. An outstanding creative arts division encom-passes programs from visual communications and recording arts technology to theater and dance. Each year it stages Tri-C Presents, a performing arts series that includes an internationally renowned jazz festival in which students have the opportunity to play with some of the world's best jazz musicians.

Whether they are enrolled in an associate's degree program, entrepreneurial training, a certificate program, or enrichment classes, Tri-C students who have earned an associate's degree are automatically accepted into Baldwin-Wallace College, or Cleveland State or Kent State (in Portage County) universities, thanks to dual admission agreements. A similar agreement with Berklee College of Music in Boston makes for a seamless transfer for jazz studies students, although many go on to the Juilliard School, Oberlin College, and other leading conservatories.

A variety of technical colleges and workforce development centers, from Ohio Technical College in Cleveland to the Cuyahoga County Employment Connection, makes up another integral component of the educational system. Perhaps the most comprehensive of these schools—and certainly the most unique for its focus on students of all ages (even K–12)—is the Cuyahoga Valley Career Center (CVCC) in Brecksville. Leaders of eight public school districts in Cuyahoga and

Summit counties came up with the idea for the center in 1972, and now those eight communities can access career education that ranges from field trips and summer camp experiences, such as the "Underwater Robot" and "Beautiful You" camp, to certificate and college-credit classes and corporate training. For high schoolers, the program combines a half-day of technical experience at CVCC with a half-day of academics at their home school. Students at the center even learn to provide services directly to the community through such on-campus sites as the cosmetology salon, restaurant, and horticulture classroom, where they sell the plants they've grown.

A high regard for education runs deep in Cuyahoga County. The Ohio Department of Education reported in August 2009 that 13 of the county's public school districts ranked as "excellent with distinction" based on state standards, which are among the highest in the nation. As students in those districts graduate, many of them remain in Greater Cleveland to attend college or take positions in the workforce. Along with graduates of the region's renowned colleges and universities who settle in Greater Cleveland, they play an important role in creating an ever-improving quality of life for themselves and future generations. As for those who choose to leave the area, they take the incomparable richness of a Greater Cleveland education with them into the world.

Opposite page: It's never too late to attend college, as this 78-year-old student at Cleveland State University proves. Center: BMW Training Center at the Ohio Technical College. This page, right: Students refine their welding skills at Cuyahoga Valley Career Center.

Energy, Transportation, and Professional Services
THE HIGH ROAD

Building on its enviable geographic location and strong infrastructure, the Greater Cleveland area has embraced innovation and new technology in both energy and transportation. Supported by strong financial institutions and professional services, area businesses are well-positioned to take advantage of capital investment programs and other private-public collaborations.

Energy

Wind, solar, and other alternative energy sources are being aggressively explored in Ohio. Ranked second in the potential for manufacturing wind turbines and components, the state is poised to take advantage of the economic development opportunities derived from wind power. The Lake Erie Energy Development Corp. (LEEDCo) reached an agreement with General Electric Co. to supply five turbines for a $100 million demonstration project in Lake Erie. Clustered six miles or so off Cleveland's shore, the 225-ton turbines would stand 300 feet above the lake and generate 20 megawatts, enough to power up to 16,000 homes. The project is the first phase of a 10-year plan to build more than 200 turbines in the lake by 2020, generating a total of 1,000 megawatts.

CHAPTERFIVE

"It's not like going to the moon," LEEDCo president Lorry Wagner acknowledged, "but it's a difficult challenge." To address such problems as how to anchor the towers and deliver the power to shore, Great Lakes Energy Institute at Case Western University is conducting innovative wind studies, including ground-breaking research on freshwater wind turbines.

Access to alternative sources of energy will enable utilities to provide cheaper, more efficient power for their millions of customers. With a goal of providing lower utility costs to families and businesses in Northeast Ohio, Northeast Ohio Public Energy Council entered an agreement with FirstEnergy Solutions Corp. (FES) to supply power for customers in 126 Northeast Ohio communities, including Cleveland. FES's Powering Our Communities program locks in long-term discounted prices to residential and small commercial customers, who could save as much as $19 million a year. FES also provides $12 million in funding support for energy-efficiency and green energy projects throughout the region. The Illuminating Company, a subsidiary of FirstEnergy, also supplies electricity to residents and businesses in Cuyahoga County.

Cleveland Public Power (CPP) provides electricity to nearly 80,000 residential, commercial, and industrial customers. CPP's 300-megawatt system ranks as the largest municipally owned electric utility in Ohio and one of the largest in the United States. Clean, efficient natural gas is delivered to customers in Cuyahoga County by Dominion Natural Gas and Columbia Gas of Ohio. WarmChoice, a weatherization program offered by Columbia Gas, provides eligible low-income customers with insulation, air sealing, and high-efficiency furnaces for their homes.

Utilities are doing their part to help create a greener future. Ten Ohio nonprofit organizations received $112,000 in Earth Day grants from Dominion Natural Gas for protecting endangered species, restoring wetlands, preserving forests, and environmental outreach. Among the recipients were Cleveland Zoological Society, WVIZ/WCPN Ideastream, Cleveland, and Habitat for Humanity.

Cleveland-area businesses are taking advantage of alternative sources of power. In 2007 Jacobs Field (now Progressive Field) became the first American League ballpark to go solar. The Cleveland Indians and Green Energy collaborated on the installation of a new solar electric system that provides 8.4 kilowatts of clean, renewable electricity.

Transportation

The Greater Cleveland area is ideally situated to serve as a transportation hub for the region and beyond. Nearly half of all U.S. households, businesses, and manufacturing plants are less than an eight-hour drive from the Cleveland area, which is served by five interstate highways and two national rail lines. Cleveland Hopkins International Airport (CLE) is within 500 miles of 43 percent of the U.S. population. Ships traverse the St. Lawrence Seaway, or Highway H_2O, to move cargo in and out of Cleveland's port.

An economic impact study released in 2010 underscored the importance of the maritime industry to the region's economy. The city's harbor and river system generate $1 billion of economic activity and more than 17,000 jobs. The third-largest port on the Great Lakes, the Cleveland-Cuyahoga County Port Authority averages 12.5 million tons of cargo per year. Nearly 4 percent of the cargo entering and leaving the port is produced or consumed with a 75-mile radius, earning the Port Authority the title of a "destination port." The Port Authority operates eight international cargo docks on 110 acres of land alongside Lake Erie on the east bank of the Cuyahoga River, while the Cleveland Bulk Terminal transshipment facility occupies 44 acres just west of the river. By spring 2011, the port could become the first international container service operating on the Great lakes, offering weekly shipping service between Cleveland and Montreal.

In an effort to become a "Green Port on a Great Lake," the Port Authority joined the Green Marine Program, a joint initiative between U.S. and Canada to preserve the Great Lakes marine environment. Scheduled for completion in 2013, this project will create a cutting-edge, sustainable port that minimizes energy use and environmental impact.

Opposite page, from left: A whale mural adorns the exterior of the Public Power Generating Station in Cleveland; power lines and a cell tower help to keep Greater Cleveland humming. This page: A pilot inspects an aircraft before takeoff at Cleveland Hopkins International Airport.

41

Cleveland Hopkins International Airport (CLE) is a hub for Continental Airlines, serving 10 million passengers every year and more than 70 destinations worldwide. During winter storms, its de-icing reclamation system speeds up ground clearance time and prevents ground water contamination. The country's first municipally owned airport, CLE is also one of the only commercial airports in the United States connected to a major NASA facility. Burke Lakefront Airport's convenient location makes it an ideal hub for the area's expanding medical industry. The Cleveland Clinic, University Hospitals, and MetroHealth use this facility to fly in out-of-state patients, organ donations, and medical specialists.

Freight travels by trail in and out of the Cleveland area on the Norfolk Southern and CSX. Serving millions of commuters each year, the Greater Cleveland Regional Transit Authority has 52 stations along the 34-mile route and provides a link between the central business district and the airport.

Financial and Professional Services

Cuyahoga County is a well-established financial center, with 30 banks reporting nearly $190 billion in assets in 2009. The Federal Reserve Bank of Cleveland, one of 12 regional Reserve Banks, serves the Fourth Federal Reserve District, which includes Ohio.

A Fortune 500 company that ranks fifth largest in the nation in deposits, PNC Financial Services Group, Inc. offers a range of services, including retail, corporate, and institutional banking. With approximately $120 billion in assets, PNC is ranked as the nation's eighth largest bank-held wealth manager by Barron's. KeyCorp, a Fortune 500 company with $100 billion in assets, ranks among the leaders in commercial banking. Fifth Third Bank, Northeastern Ohio, an affiliate of the parent company in Cincinnati, is a diversified financial services leader providing a broad spectrum of money management options.

This page: Passngers line at at the Shaker Square Station to board the RTA. Opposite page, from left: Key Tower dominates the Cleveland skyline; CBIZ headquarters

Located in gleaming new headquarters in the Galleria at Erieview, Dollar Bank is the nation's largest independent mutual bank, with assets of $5.9 billion. Other financial institutions serving the area include First Federal Savings and Loan Association, FS Financial Corporation, LNB Bancorp, Ohio Savings Bank, and PVF Capital Corporation.

When it comes to insurance, the Cleveland area is truly progressive. A Fortune 500 company headquartered in Mayfield Village, Progressive Auto Insurance offers auto, boat, motorcycle, and RV insurance to millions of customers around the country. Ohio's oldest and largest health insurance provider, Medical Mutual serves more than 1.6 million healthcare customers. Headquartered in downtown Cleveland, Medical Mutual is owned by its policyholders, not stockholders.

The Cleveland area boasts a distinguished list of professional services. One of the nation's leading architectural firms, ka Architecture, celebrated its 50th anniversary in 2010. Headquartered in Cleveland, ka designs office space for clients such as Key Bank and has developed a niche market in the expanding areas of health care and higher education. Developing shopping centers in prime locations and featuring prominent retailers is the focus of Developers

Diversified Realty Corporation. Mix-used, lifestyle, and hybrid centers, and revitalizing once-thriving malls are also found in its growing portfolio. CBIZ, Inc. provides a wide array of professional services, including tax services and financial business consulting, payroll and employee benefits services, medical practice management, valuation, and more.

Blueprint for the Future

Even when faced with the challenges posed by a recession, the Greater Cleveland area can draw upon a wealth of assets: its central geographic location, a strong transportation network, access to an educated workforce, and a strong commitment by the private and public sectors to nurture technological innovation. Entrepreneurs and innovators in advanced and alternative energy, biomedical, advanced materials, advanced propulsion, and other areas can seek assistance from the Greater Cleveland Partnership. The largest chamber of commerce in the state, with 16,000 member companies, the GCP is a major player in economic development in the region, helping to connect businesses to available resources.

Bringing great ideas from the laboratory to the marketplace is the mission of Ohio Third Frontier, a visionary initiative created in 2002. Extended through 2015, the $2.3 billion initiative supports applied research and commercialization, entrepreneurial assistance, early-stage capital formation, and expansion of a skilled talent pool. Building on strengths in technology and innovation, the initiative will help to accelerate and sustain technology-based economic growth in Cuyahoga County.

PARTNERS IN PROGRESS:
PROFILES OF COMPANIES AND ORGANIZATIONS

PART TWO

PROFILES OF COMPANIES AND ORGANIZATIONS

Featured Cities, Tourism, and Hospitality

Crowne Plaza Cleveland City Centre Hotel

Overlooking beautiful Lake Erie in the heart of Cleveland, this upscale hotel is located ideally for both business and leisure travelers, adjacent to the convention center and the city's business districts and within walking distance of some of the city's most popular attractions. This environmentally responsible hotel offers spacious accommodations, extensive amenities, and ample meeting space.

Above: The lobby of the Crowne Plaza Cleveland City Centre Hotel offers guests a taste of the excitement that they will find all around the city at attractions such as the Rock and Roll Hall of Fame.

As everyone knows, "Cleveland Rocks!" And at the center of the action is the Crowne Plaza Cleveland City Centre Hotel. Surrounded not only by major attractions but by the corporate offices of some of the world's largest companies, the Crowne Plaza is the ideal place to stay whether for business or for pleasure. Affording spectacular views of Lake Erie and the North Coast Harbor District, the hotel is adjacent to the Cleveland Convention Center and two blocks from the Rock and Roll Hall of Fame and the Great Lakes Science Center. Within walking distance are the Historic Warehouse District, with its wealth of entertainment, and

PlayhouseSquare, the nation's second-largest performing arts center. Also a short walk away are Progressive Field, home to baseball's Cleveland Indians; Browns Stadium, home to the Cleveland Browns football team; and Quicken Loans Arena, known as the Q, home court of basketball's Cleveland Cavaliers. Among the many other nearby attractions are the Metroparks Zoo, the Cleveland Museum of Art, and the NASA Glenn Research Center.

The Crowne Plaza is within blocks of the corporate offices of such giants as Deloitte & Touche, AT&T, Ernst & Young, Eaton Corporation, Sherwin Williams, and many others. It is also one block from the Anthony J. Celebrezze Federal Building and less than 13 miles from Cleveland Hopkins International Airport.

The hotel's scenic and strategic location makes it the ideal place for a meeting, conference, or social event. Through the Crowne Plaza Meetings Success Program, the hotel partners with the client to ensure each event's success by assigning a Crowne Meeting Director to serve as the single point of contact. Crowne Meeting Directors are true professionals who facilitate the planning process and satisfy even last-minute or unusual requests. With the Crowne Plaza's 2-Hour Response Guarantee, each client requesting meeting information receives a response within two hours and a complete proposal by the next business day. Once the event begins, the Crowne Meeting Director provides the client with a Daily Meeting Debrief, an itemized account of that day's expenditures. In addition, all guestrooms, meeting rooms, and hotel public areas are equipped with high-speed, wireless Internet access. The hotel also offers a complete business center that provides computer access and photocopy, transparency, and fax services all day every day.

With more than 27,000 square feet of flexible meeting space, the hotel can accommodate any kind of event. On the lobby level, the 4,000-square-foot Dorothy Fuldheim Ballroom serves as a dining room or theater for up to 250 people and as a classroom for up to 110 people, and accommodates up to 27 eight-by-eight-foot

exhibits. On the sixth floor is the 9,040-square-foot Grand Ballroom, which includes a beautiful built-in double-sided bar, dance floor, and pre-function space and accommodates up to 1,025 people, depending on the event. On the same floor are four breakout rooms ranging in size from 940 to 1,980 square feet and accommodating between 45 and 250 people and up to 14 exhibits. An additional 12 meeting rooms ranging in size from 300 to 560 square feet are found on the seventh floor; the 675-square-foot Executive Board Room is on the 22nd floor and overlooks Lake Erie.

Dining at the Crowne Plaza is also a memorable experience. The menu at Pimentos Restaurant and Lounge "rocks" with such signature dishes as Peter, Paul, and Mary Crab Cakes; Pound of McCartney's Wings; and Mick's Brown Sugar, Honey, and Bourbon Barbecue Ribs. For a late bite, the Green Olive Martini Bar offers cocktails, sandwiches, and snacks.

After a day of business meetings or sightseeing, guests of the Crowne Plaza appreciate the benefits of the Sleep Advantage Program®. Plush duvets, fluffy pillows, satin-soft cotton sheets, eye masks, earplugs, and lavender mist—and, upon request, QuietZone floors—all make for a restful night's sleep. All 472 guest

rooms come with free high-speed Internet access, voice mail, CD player, hairdryer, coffeemaker, and iron and ironing board. Other hotel amenities include same-day dry cleaning and laundry service, a full-service hair salon, and a 24-hour fitness room with state-of-the-art equipment.

As one of Cleveland's most important and influential corporate citizens, the Crowne Plaza is proud to support the Convention and Visitors Bureau of Cleveland, known as Positively Cleveland, in its Sustainable Destination Initiative. By incorporating green practices into its operations, the hotel is setting an example of environmental sustainability for the hospitality industry. Among the measures the hotel has taken are recycling paper, cardboard, computer equipment, and toner and inkjet cartridges; installing energy-efficient lightbulbs; using green cleaning products; and offering a subsidy for hotel employees who ride the bus to and from work.

Deluxe accommodations, excellent event facilities, unbeatable location, and environmental responsibility are four reasons why the Crowne Plaza Cleveland City Centre "rocks." Additional information is available on the hotel's Web site at www.clevelanddowntownhotel.com.

Above: With its prime downtown location, the Crowne Plaza Cleveland City Centre Hotel is the perfect setting for a convention, event conference, or gathering. With 27,000 square feet of flexible meeting space and 20 separate function rooms, the hotel offers facilities for meetings of all types, from corporate luncheons to elegant galas.

City of Solon

A long history of innovative and successful economic development programs reflects this city's deft hand when it comes to supporting its existing businesses and welcoming new ones, attracting business locally, nationally, and globally. With a proactive economic development department, a strong relationship with local companies, and an enviable quality of life, the city is a star in the northeastern Ohio business firmament.

Above left: Solon City Hall is home to city government, including the City of Solon Planning and Economic Development Department. Above center: The Solon Philharmonic Orchestra performs at the Solon Center for the Arts. Above right: Among the facilities provided by the City of Solon Recreation Department is the Solon Community Center. The department offers recreation programs for all ages. Opposite page: Solon is home to Nestlé Prepared Foods Company.

Business has a friend in Solon. This city has been an economic development leader since the 1950s, when policymakers recognized the relationship between a thriving business community and a thriving quality of life. Championing economic development in the decades that followed, the City of Solon has become a model for attracting and retaining business.

"When It Gets Down to Business, Solon Gets It!" is Solon's marketing slogan. Backing up this statement is the city's Economic Development Plan, which elucidates the programs created to support existing enterprises and attract new ones, including job creation grants, tax abatement, and regular visits with business executives. When the economic development association for northeast Ohio—Team NEO—joined with *Inside Business* magazine in 2007 to create an awards program honoring organizations that make an impact on economic development, the City of Solon was a winner. The city's Growth & Revitalization Incentive Program (GRIP)—which offers grants to property owners who improve industrial or commercial buildings—was recognized for its value in strengthening business presence in the region.

Developing international trade is also a key provision of the Economic Development Plan. Solon's two-pronged strategy involves assisting local business owners in becoming globally competitive and attracting investment to the city from abroad.

The Solon International Roundtable, a partnership between the Solon Chamber of Commerce and the city, is a forum to assist local businesses through mentoring, education, and providing contacts related to global trade. The city builds alliances with regional economic development organizations and enlists members of its internationally diverse residential and business population to help recruit companies abroad that may be interested in locating in the area.

The excellent quality of life in Solon is a major factor in companies' decisions to locate to and expand in Solon. Solon City Schools, one of Ohio's top school districts, provides local children with an outstanding education. Abundant recreational activities are offered in Solon's parks and state-of-the-art Community Center. The city has a stellar arts scene, which includes the popular Solon Center for the Arts. These amenities contributed to Solon's national ranking of number 23 in *Money Magazine*'s Best Places to Live 2009 for small towns in the United States. The City of Solon provides additional information on its Web site at www.solonohio.org.

Hampton Inn Cleveland–Solon

Situated in an upscale community in the Cleveland metropolitan area, this hospitality landmark is renowned for its personal service and warm, friendly atmosphere. With clean, comfortable guest rooms and amenities ranging from complimentary hot buffet breakfasts to free wireless high-speed Internet access, the hotel strives to make every guest, whether business traveler or vacationer, feel welcome.

full kitchen, a living room, and a whirlpool spa. There is no need to miss favorite television shows while traveling, as each room is equipped with cable television, including free Home Box Office (HBO) and ESPN, as well as pay-per-view movies. Beyond these features, amenities include coffeemakers, hair dryers, ironing boards and irons, and same-day laundry and valet service. Specially accessible guest rooms are available for people who have disabilities.

Staff members at Hampton Inn Cleveland–Solon recognize that for guests, a successful trip, whether for business or pleasure, takes energy. To ensure that no one goes out the door in the morning hungry, a complimentary hot breakfast buffet is waiting in the dining room daily. The manager hosts a reception Monday through Thursday evenings for those who check in during the week, and whenever guests check in,

Top left: The Hampton Inn Cleveland–Solon is highly rated. Above left: The hotel's van provides guests with complimentary shuttle service to local destinations. Above right: The hotel is noted for its inviting ambience.

A good hotel can be as simple as a place to have a restful night's sleep or as enticing as a home away from home—a place for relaxation, exercise, and entertainment. The Hampton Inn Cleveland–Solon is both—and more.

Ranked number one in the city in 2009 by TripAdvisor visitors, who share their firsthand experiences, the Hampton Inn Cleveland–Solon also was a 2006 winner of the Solon Chamber of Commerce Business of the Year award. When so many people agree, it is a sure sign that something positive is going on.

The hotel is located in the heart of the upscale Solon business district, within walking distance of restaurants and theaters. Its 103 spacious guest rooms have either king-size beds or two double beds, and special two-room suites also feature a

freshly baked cookies are available. And at the Hampton Inn Cleveland–Solon, pets are always welcome.

The staff is serious about providing amenities that make a difference, and the hotel, upgraded in 2007, has what it takes. Business travelers appreciate the meeting space available in two well-appointed conference rooms. Complimentary wireless high-speed Internet access is available in every guest room, and a complimentary hotel van is on call to shuttle guests to and from local businesses, attractions, and other destinations, which include a 24-hour business center.

When it is time to work muscles and release endorphins, an on-site, state-of-the-art exercise room and indoor swimming pool do the trick. The pool, surrounded by

windows overlooking lush landscaping, gives swimmers a pleasing sense of nature regardless of the temperature outside.

The motto of staff members at the Hampton Inn Cleveland–Solon is "We Love Having You Here." And they do. The attractive, comfortable atmosphere is proof. Under the leadership of the hotel's general manager, Donna Doberstyn, the staff focuses on exceeding the expectations of guests.

The ambience is a clear reflection of the general manager's experience in the hospitality industry. Before moving to another town, Doberstyn served for 16 years as manager of a local hotel. When the Hampton Inn was opened in Solon in 1997, she was eager to return and accepted the position of general manager in 1998. Working with sales director Ewa Antonczyk, Doberstyn was able to attract and develop a hospitality team that is among the best. Staff members have proven time and again that they sincerely care about their guests and their community. For two years in a row, 2007 and 2008, the hotel received from its management company, New Castle Hotels & Resorts, the prestigious Best Overall Performance Award for hotels of under 150 rooms.

Charitable contributions are key to the culture at Hampton Inn Cleveland–Solon. To give back to the community that has been so good for business, the hotel participates in a variety of events such as the annual Solon Home Days parade in July. Year after year, hotel staff members distribute candy and beach balls to children along the parade route. During the holiday season, as part of a local adopt-a-family program the hotel donates to a deserving family a suite for a weekend, along with all meals and tickets to a movie.

Complimentary guest rooms are regularly provided for businesses, organizations, and schools in the community, and meeting space is made available to the Solon Chamber of Commerce. Girl Scouts and Boy Scouts receive lotions and shampoo from the hotel, and Valley Save-A-Pet is given bedsheets and mattress pads for the animals' sleeping quarters.

The Hampton Inn Cleveland–Solon, a member of the Hilton Family of Hotels, provides additional information about its facilities and services on its Web site at www.solonhamptoninn.com.

Top left: Guests appreciate the hotel's heated indoor swimming pool. Above left: Each day, a complimentary hot breakfast buffet awaits guests in the dining room. Above right: Well-appointed guest rooms feature a king-size bed or two double beds.

Crowne Plaza Hotel–Cleveland Airport

Just minutes from downtown Cleveland and one shuttle stop from Cleveland Hopkins International Airport, this upscale, modern, award-winning hotel received a multimillion-dollar renovation in 2007. The hotel provides a full complement of guest amenities and promises "a better meeting experience for all meeting planners and a better night's sleep for meeting attendees and all guests."

Above: The first-class Crowne Plaza Hotel–Cleveland Airport offers a location for travelers that is convenient to not only the airport but also downtown businesses and local attractions.

In Middleburg Heights in southwest Cleveland, at the heart of the Tri-City area of Middleburg Heights, Berea, and Brook Park, the Crowne Plaza Hotel–Cleveland Airport is an ideal place to meet. Here, guests find all the amenities of a downtown hotel with the added convenience of proximity to a major airport. In fact, Cleveland Hopkins International Airport is just 3.5 miles away and is accessible by a complimentary shuttle, while downtown Cleveland is only minutes away by car. Within walking distance of the hotel are restaurants, movie theaters, and the Cleveland Metropolitan Parks System—MetroParks—a set of public parks that forms a large ring known as the Emerald Necklace around the city. Additional entertainment venues and two large shopping malls are a short drive away. The

hotel also is close to the NASA Glenn Research Center, the Cleveland International Exposition and Convention Center, Baldwin-Wallace College, and Southwest General Health Center. A hotel does not make its reputation by location alone, of course; it must also offer immaculate facilities, elegant accommodations, and exceptional service. The Crowne Plaza Hotel provides all of these and more. In 2007 the hotel underwent a multimillion-dollar renovation of the entire premises.

The Crowne Plaza Hotel–Cleveland Airport was awarded the 2008 Renovation Award by the InterContinental Hotels Group (the world's largest hotel group by number of rooms). Also, Gary W. Starr, mayor of Middleburg Heights, proclaimed November 7, 2008, to be Crowne Plaza Day and honored the hotel with the city's 2008 Renovation Award. In addition, the Crowne Plaza Hotel was honored by the Middleburg Heights Chamber of Commerce with its 2008 Best Interior Renovation Award.

A Better Meeting Experience

With more than 16,000 square feet of flexible meeting space, the Crowne Plaza Hotel is able to accommodate virtually any type of event, from business conferences to conventions, to educational seminars to wedding receptions. The hotel's 14 meeting and banquet rooms range in size from 480 to nearly 7,000 square feet. The majority of the meeting rooms can be configured to accommodate anywhere from as few as 12 people to, in the Grand Ballroom, as many as 800. In addition, there are two tiered amphitheaters: the Superior, with seating for 60, and the Ontario, which seats 40. State-of-the-art audiovisual and telecommunications equipment is provided to support successful presentations.

Providing the site and equipment is just one aspect of the hotel's meeting services. With the Crowne Plaza Hotel's Two-Hour Response Guarantee, initial inquiries about meeting and event planning are addressed within two business hours, and a proposal is provided by the next business day. A Crowne Meetings Director then works with the client to plan, coordinate, and execute the meeting. The Director is the

sole contact with the client, easing communication, eliminating confusion, and ensuring that all arrangements are satisfactory. To help meeting planners manage their budget, the hotel provides a Daily Meetings Debrief, which itemizes all accounting for that day's expenditures. Clients who enroll in the Crowne Plaza Hotel's Priority Club Meeting Rewards program receive three points for every U.S. dollar spent on qualified meetings. The points, which never expire, may be redeemed for merchandise certificates, airline miles, free hotel nights, or savings on future meetings.

The Sleep Advantage

The Crowne Plaza Hotel's excellent meeting accommodations are matched by its luxurious guest accommodations and amenities. The Crowne Plaza Sleep Advantage program features comfortable beds with plush duvets and sleep amenities. A Quiet Zone floor, additional guest room amenities, and a guaranteed wake-up call are provided to assure comfort and satisfaction. Each of the hotel's smoke-free 238 guest rooms and suites feature a coffeemaker, clock radio, CD player, iron and ironing board, hair dryer, telephone with voice mail, 32-inch flatscreen cable/satellite television, and free Home Box Office (HBO). Priority Club Rewards are offered as a "thank you" to the hotel's loyal guests. As with Club Meeting Rewards, the points acquired through Priority Club Rewards never expire and may be used for miles, merchandise, hotel stays, and more.

Additional On-Site Amenities for Guests

Other guest amenities include free parking, complimentary airport shuttle, a sundry shop open 24 hours a day, a fully equipped 24-hour business center for guests' office or personal needs, and high-speed Internet access and wireless data connection available throughout the hotel.

Guests also enjoy the excellent cuisine at Bucci's at the Crowne Plaza Hotel. This renowned restaurant, with many locations in the Cleveland region, serves breakfast, lunch, and dinner, and offers a late-night bar menu. Specialties include bacon-wrapped barbecued shrimp; the restaurant's legendary Parmesan specialties made with veal, chicken, or eggplant; plus steaks and pork chop Milanese. The restaurant also provides catering for events at the hotel. Bucci's Lounge provides an elegant spot for relaxing after a day of meetings, while those looking for a workout head for the on-site fitness center, which features universal, treadmill, and elliptical equipment. The hotel's indoor swimming pool and sauna offer both exercise and relaxation.

The Crowne Plaza Hotel–Cleveland Airport provides additional information about its guest rooms, amenities, dining, meeting services, and more on its Web site at www.crowneplaza.com/clevelandarpt.

Above left: Guest rooms and suites at the Crowne Plaza Hotel provide luxuriant and comfortable settings that offer full amenities.

Hilton Garden Inn Cleveland Downtown

Centrally located in Downtown Cleveland's historic Gateway District, this hotel boasts luxurious and work-friendly accommodations, complemented by a wide range of conveniences. Spacious guest rooms, extensive amenities, outstanding event space, and a prime location in the heart of the city make this hotel an excellent choice for both the business and the pleasure traveler.

Boasting one of the best locations in Cleveland and one of the most respected names in the hospitality industry, the elegant Hilton Garden Inn Cleveland Downtown offers 240 spacious guest rooms, including eight two-room suites, all designed with comfort and convenience in mind. Offering a choice of a king bed or two queen beds, each room features the new Garden Sleep System® bed, which self-adjusts to each guest's mattress comfort preference. Furnishings also include granite countertops and vanities, an armchair and ottoman, a large work desk, and a Herman Miller Mirra® ergonomic desk chair. The beautiful décor is complemented by a full range of amenities, including complimentary wired and wireless high-speed Internet access, voice mail, a data port, and two telephones, each with a separate line. Rooms also feature a refrigerator, microwave, coffeemaker, and hairdryer, air-conditioning, and a 32-inch, high-definition, flat-screen television with cable, pay-per-view, and HBO, CNN, and ESPN. In addition, the hotel offers a fitness center and an indoor swimming pool equipped with a whirlpool. Dining options include an upscale sports-style bar, a restaurant, and evening room service.

The Hilton Garden Inn is an excellent venue for meetings and other business or social

Photos, both pages: A great location, tasteful furnishings, clean and comfortable rooms, and a friendly staff make the Hilton Garden Inn Cleveland Downtown a top choice among travelers.

events. It features the 20,000-square-foot Gateway Conference Center, which includes the 5,500-square-foot Carnegie Ballroom, both renovated spaces that include elements from their original 1922 construction combined with attractive contemporary features. The conference center comprises three ballrooms and a banquet room as well as eight meeting rooms. The adjacent Carnegie Ballroom accommodates up to 550 guests and offers views of Progressive Field and downtown Cleveland. Business travelers also appreciate the hotel's two fully equipped, 24-hour complimentary business centers.

The hotel's luxurious accommodations and excellent meeting facilities are matched by a convenient and accessible location at the gateway to downtown off Interstates 71, 77, and 90. The hotel is directly across from Progressive Field—home of the Cleveland Indians—and within walking distance of Quicken Loans Arena, Cleveland Browns Stadium, Cleveland State University's Wolstein Center, the Rock and Roll Hall of Fame and Museum, and the Playhouse Square theater district. The Hilton Garden Inn Cleveland Downtown does indeed offer "Everything. Right where you need it."

Further information is available on the hotel's Web site at www.clevelanddowntown.stayhgi.com.

PROFILES OF COMPANIES AND ORGANIZATIONS
Architecture and Development

ka Architecture

Since 1960 this Cleveland architectural firm has provided knowledgeable and experienced service to developers, owners, and institutions nationwide. Together its architects, planners, landscape architects, interior designers, and graphic designers have built an extensive portfolio of projects including retail centers, mixed-use developments, corporate office buildings, and high-rise residential complexes.

The ka Architecture Story

"How do you start an architectural practice? You get fired!" These were the prophetic words uttered by Keeva J. Kekst after he was given a choice by his employer to continue working for them or to consider a major residential commission he was offered personally. Kekst chose to start his own firm in the attic of his home. This attic-room start-up quickly grew into a bustling downtown office on Euclid Avenue, where Kekst could "practice with the big boys."

Four years after leaving behind that attic office, Kekst was introduced to the Edward J. DeBartolo Co., then the nation's largest mall developer. This relationship, along with Kekst's tenacity and determination, resulted in Kekst's company being awarded the architectural commission for the Richmond Mall Shopping Center near Cleveland. A month later, Kekst was also awarded a contract to design a regional shopping mall in Bowling Green, Kentucky. The acquisition of these two retail projects marked the beginning of the firm's commercial real estate endeavors. The emphasis over time was on serving the developer community based on coming to understand the developer's needs and business model. Commissions for multifamily, residential, nursing homes, industrial buildings, and civic, educational, and religious facilities followed, greatly expanding the company's breadth of capabilities and its client base. Keeva J. Kekst Architects evolved into a national practice, committed to creating quality architecture by serving its clients and making their requirements the focus of the company's work.

Through the 1970s and 1980s, the firm continued to grow, becoming registered in 44 states and Puerto Rico and eventually changing its name to ka Architecture. The office moved to the historic Western Reserve Building in the Warehouse District, where the company is headquartered today. In 1989 ka was the 18th-largest architectural firm in the nation, and its client list included some of the most successful retail developers in the country. During the 1990s, ka began serving regional corporate clients as an outgrowth of a successful interior design practice. Many clients found ka's knowledge of the speculative office mindset to be an asset to corporate end users, who were looking to gain flexibility within and create multiple uses of a corporate building. ka continued to serve other markets, earning commissions for medical office buildings, multifamily housing, and major department stores.

ka in the New Millennium

Transitioning into its third generation of ownership, ka celebrated its 50th anniversary in 2010. Since its inception, ka has gone on to complete more than 75 regional shopping malls, over 300 department stores, and numerous "open-air" lifestyle centers nationwide. ka has also been instrumental in many mall renovations, some of which were originally designed by ka, such as the Richmond Town Square, formerly Richmond Mall Shopping Center. Breathing new life into outdated retail centers of all kinds is yet another way ka has been able to help developer/owners.

Above left: ka Architecture provided architectural, interior, and graphic design services for the Icon in the Gulch, a unique mixed-use development in downtown Nashville. Above right: Allen-Bradley chose ka to design its regional headquarters for this subsidiary of Rockwell Automation, in Mayfield Heights, Ohio. ka provided the master planning and landscape architecture and served as the design and executive architect for the project.

ka's in-depth knowledge in all types of retail venues also made the company a natural choice for developers of mixed-use projects in which the retail component is vital to the success of the project. As mixed-use projects are geographically diverse, **ka** traveled to various locations such as the Westfield San Francisco Centre in San Francisco, California, and the Annapolis Town Center at Parole in Annapolis, Maryland.

Another component of mixed-use projects is commercial office space. **ka** has designed more than 10 million square feet of commercial office space, either as speculative office space or single end–user office space for corporate clients. Working for national companies such as Eaton, IMG, MBNA, Booz Allen Hamilton, KeyCorp, Progressive Insurance, ICI Paints, Avery Dennison, and Rockwell Automation has given **ka** the opportunity to earn a reputation as a trusted partner.

Multifamily residential projects have had a significant place in **ka**'s history, with most recent additions to the company's portfolio inclusive of the Icon and Velocity in the Gulch, neighboring residences in Nashville, Tennessee. The firm has completed a substantial number of continuing-care retirement community projects and recently began working in the area of university student housing. As colleges look to increase enrollment and become more attractive to potential registrants, student housing has become a fast growing real estate market. **ka**'s background in multifamily housing and its appreciation of the needs of the residential developer adapt well to this niche market.

A Half Century of Experience

With more than five decades of service to the development community, **ka** has become more than just the quarterback who assembles and leads its team of designers, engineers, and other consultants to deliver a superior set of plans from which the general contractor can construct an exemplary project. Today **ka** often finds itself making critical introductions between land owners and potential developers that result in partnerships; between tenants and landlords that help cement a development's success; or even between lenders looking to place financing or communities looking to spur growth or redevelopment and to developers in search of financing or looking to participate in a public-private partnership. What any of these people will say, and what all its past clients will attest to, is that **ka** is a great team player.

ka also recognizes that sustainability is a priority in new construction and often uses it to lower operating costs. Leadership in Energy and Environmental Design accredited professionals (LEED–APs) make up more than 30 percent of **ka**'s staff, an advantage that the company uses to incorporate the principles of green design throughout the project process, from sensitive site planning to design of energy-efficient building systems. A longtime member and sponsor of the U.S. Green Building Coalition, **ka** became certified as an Energy Star Partner through the U.S. Environmental Protection Agency and Department of Energy in 2008. As executive architect on The Promenade Bolingbrook in Illinois, one of the first retail LEED-certified projects in the country, **ka** helped the developer attain its sustainability goals.

ka's depth of knowledge and vast experience provide its clients with a level of service that generates better tenants, higher patronage, and thus greater returns on their investment. **ka**'s commitment to architectural internship and continuing education is what will keep the organization ahead of the curve for decades to come. Additional information is available on **ka** Architecture's Web site at www. **ka**inc.com.

Above left: **ka** served as the retail design and executive architect and The Martin Architectural Group served as the master planning architect for Greenberg Gibbons Commercial Corporation's Annapolis Towne Centre at Parole, a 32-acre mixed-use center in Annapolis, Maryland. Above center: Forest City Development and Westfield Corporation retained **ka** as executive architect for its Westfield San Francisco Centre, a 1.5 million-square-foot mixed-use historic preservation in downtown San Francisco. Above right: **ka** designed The Shops at Fallen Timbers in Maumee, Ohio, for General Growth Properties, Inc.

PROFILES OF COMPANIES AND ORGANIZATIONS
Education

Cuyahoga Community College (Tri-C®)

For almost 50 years, this college has served the changing educational and training needs of the diverse local community. With a proud tradition of helping people build their future and improve their quality of life, Cuyahoga Community College (Tri-C®) offers quality education that is both affordable and accessible to all Northeast Ohio residents.

Since its founding in 1963, Cuyahoga Community College (Tri-C®) has served the residents of Northeast Ohio, providing affordable, accessible education to those seeking career advancement and the opportunity for a better life. Tri-C knows that an educated and trained workforce is critical to the viability and competitiveness of the region. Providing opportunities for both personal and community transformation, Tri-C offers university transfer, technical, and lifelong learning programs with flexible schedules at affordable prices. The college also offers career exploration and advancement initiatives, hands-on workforce training, and high school partnerships for student success.

Nationally recognized as one of the country's most technologically advanced two-year colleges, Tri-C was a founding member of the prestigious League for Innovation in the Community College, a consortium of 19 of the most innovative two-year colleges in the nation. The college's state-of-the art facilities and programs support and promote technology, helping its students succeed in an increasingly technological economy.

Tri-C serves students through multiple campus locations and facilities:

- The **Metropolitan Campus** in Downtown Cleveland offers leading-edge health careers laboratories, is home to the nationally renowned Tri-C JazzFest Cleveland®, and features industry-standard laboratories in programs such as Recording Arts and Technology and Hospitality Management.
- The **Center for Nursing and Health Careers**, located on the Metropolitan Campus, utilizes state-of-the-art technology and offers a simulated 22-bed hospital unit, theater-style classrooms with observation technology, and practical hands-on and clinical experience.
- The **Eastern Campus** in Highland Hills offers a 600-seat performing arts center and features state-of-the-art classrooms and laboratories for programs such as Plant Science and Landscape Design and Visual Communication Design, plus a Massotherapy student clinic that is open to the public.
- The **Western Campus** in Parma offers an exceptional learning environment with a hands-on Health Careers and Sciences building; an advanced automotive technology center; a fire tower where Fire Academy and Technology students hone their skills; and a Visual Communication Center of Excellence that offers courses in photography, multimedia, graphic arts, commercial art and design, and Web publishing.
- The **Unified Technologies Center (UTC),** home of the Tri-C Workforce Solutions division, offers training in advanced manufacturing and engineering, logistics and supply-chain management, public safety, alternative energy and sustainability, and career development resources. It is also the site of the Louis Stokes

Telecommunications Center, which offers access to satellite transmission from anywhere in the world.

- **Corporate College**® is designed for individuals, as well as businesses, that are seeking to improve skills and boost knowledge to compete in today's business world. Programs include high-end technology courses and a wide spectrum of leadership and professional development programs.

Tri-C enjoys strong community support and collaborates with many industries and institutions in Northeast Ohio. It also offers scholarships and educational program development and enhancement to help bridge any financial gaps for students.

"Cuyahoga Community College is privileged and honored to serve our community," says Jerry Sue Thornton, Ph.D., president of Tri-C. "Tri-C has earned a well-deserved national and local reputation for being efficient, effective, accessible, innovative, and responsive to the changing needs of those it serves."

A key participant in enhancing the economic climate of greater Cleveland and the Northeast Ohio region, Tri-C is a large local employer and major purchaser of goods and services. Tri-C also generates significant economic activity in the form of student education-related spending and draws millions in pension dollars back into the local economy.

Carrying on its tradition of quality education that is both affordable and accessible, Tri-C continues to imagine, innovate, and shape and enrich the lives of Northeast Ohio residents. The college is making learning even more accessible and effective by offering nearly 1,000 credit courses online in order to suit students' busy lifestyles. By continually assessing how effectively the college is meeting emerging community needs, Tri-C will ensure that students are prepared to succeed in the ever-changing global workplace.

Additional information is available on the Tri-C Web site at www.tri-c.edu.

Above left: Nursing students walk by the human patient simulator laboratory at the college's Metropolitan Campus Center for Nursing and Health Careers. Tri-C is a national leader in health careers education. Above right: Each semester Tri-C offers more than 1,000 for-credit courses in more than 140 career and technical programs and liberal arts curricula.

Cuyahoga Valley Career Center

Providing valuable guidance, services, and resources to a diverse student body, this center assists students of all ages in achieving their career-related goals. With hands-on programs, experienced instructors, current technology, and job search assistance, Cuyahoga Valley Career Center helps people enter, compete, and advance in an ever-changing work world. CVCC truly delivers on its tagline, 'Need skills? Ours *WORK*!'

Above: Cuyahoga Valley Career Center students represent a variety of career-technical industries.

Established in 1972 in Brecksville, Ohio, by eight public school districts in Cuyahoga and Summit counties, Cuyahoga Valley Career Center (CVCC) helps students navigate today's global workplace in an advanced-technology school. Designed to educate and to serve students in career and technical education, planning, and development processes, CVCC offers services and resources that help students cultivate and enhance skills and allow them to explore career options, master job-search techniques and strategies, and research employment and college opportunities. With technologically advanced programs and equipment, CVCC provides the strong foundation that today's employers seek and colleges enjoy. CVCC students annually receive state and national recognition for their skills achievements.

CVCC annually serves tens of thousands of kindergarten through twelfth-grade students, adults, customers, and employers through its variety of daytime, evening, and weekend educational programs and community services. It offers career and technical high school programs, adult education, and career development. The CVCC school of nursing offers both full- and part-time programs.

CVCC prepares its students to make informed career choices and positions them for future success by providing age-appropriate resources and relevant experiences. Elementary through high school students learn about careers and gain skills to help them compete in a global economy. Seventh through ninth graders can attend summer career camps. High school juniors and seniors can choose from 30 career and technical programs that include rigorous academics. CVCC instructors have years of experience in their fields and provide students with real workplace training and experiences. Students who complete programs at CVCC can enter college and apprenticeships or go directly into the workforce upon graduation.

CVCC's certification and workforce-development programs are designed to correspond to job opportunities within the community. Adult education courses provide current technology, experienced instructors, industry credentials, flexible schedules, affordable training, and job search assistance in a convenient location. Ongoing registration is offered for classes that start each month, helping adult students remain competitive in today's workforce. CVCC offers training programs in areas that are in demand by Northeast Ohio employers, providing a highly skilled workforce to support the region's economic development. CVCC is part of the University System of Ohio, enabling adult students to earn college credit by completing career courses that are approved by the Ohio Board of Regents.

CVCC provides job placement services for employers, current students, and graduates, using state-of-the-art methods to link employers with candidates who meet their needs. Job-search training seminars and job coaching help students develop the skills necessary to obtain employment. CVCC provides personalized career coaching and job-search support for its graduates throughout their careers.

Additional information about CVCC's programs and services is available on its Web site at www.cvccworks.com.

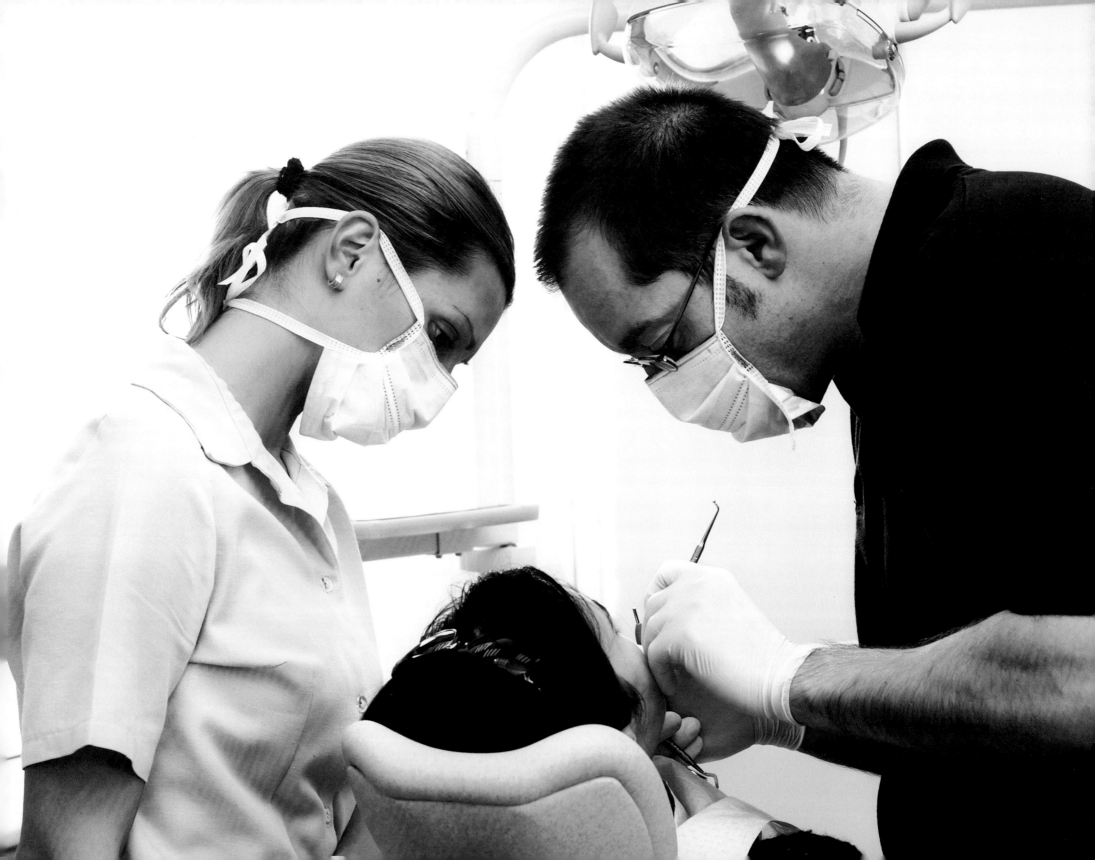

John Carroll University

John Carroll University educates the whole person—intellectually, spiritually, emotionally, and physically—in keeping with its Jesuit mission. Students can pursue a bachelor's degree in more than 40 academic programs through the College of Arts and Sciences and the Boler School of Business, or a master's degree in more than 20 graduate programs. A 15:1 student-faculty ratio ensures individual attention and an interactive experience.

Right: John Carroll University's 60-acre campus is distinguished by its striking Gothic architecture and beautiful landscaping. At the heart of it is The Quad, where students greet each other on their way to class, relax in the sun, or play pick-up lacrosse, football, or soccer.

Photo: © Don Hammerman

easy access to restaurants, museums, professional sports team venues, parks and recreational sites, and meaningful community service opportunities in and around Cleveland.

The university consists of the College of Arts and Sciences, the John M. and Mary Jo Boler School of Business, and more than 20 graduate programs. For more than two decades, *U.S. News & World Report* has ranked John Carroll among the top 10 of the Midwest's universities that grant master's degrees. The university's Boler School of Business and accounting program are both accredited by the Association to Advance Collegiate Schools of Business—a double distinction held by only 11 percent of business schools worldwide.

John Carroll students are keenly aware that the world also is their classroom. The university offers study abroad and service-based immersion programs that take many of its students around the globe for semester, summer, or semester-break trips.

As one of 28 Jesuit Catholic colleges and universities in the United States, John Carroll University inspires individuals to excel in learning, leadership, and service. John Carroll is consistently one of the top schools in the Midwest for graduation and retention rates. In fact, its graduation rates significantly exceed U.S. and Ohio averages.

John Carroll's location in University Heights, Ohio, affords its 3,800 students the best of both suburban and urban worlds: a beautiful, safe campus tucked into a neighborhood of tree-lined streets and lovely homes, combined with

Students provide exemplary service to communities. John Carroll students are on the U.S. President's Higher Education Community Service Honor Roll, which annually recognizes institutions of higher education for their commitment to and achievement in community service.

Founded as Saint Ignatius College in 1886, the school was renamed John Carroll University in 1923 to honor America's first Catholic bishop, John Carroll of Maryland. John Carroll University provides additional information on its Web site at www.jcu.edu.

PROFILES OF COMPANIES AND ORGANIZATIONS

Financial, Business, and Technology Services

KeyBank

This lender, leader, and economic catalyst, headquartered in Cleveland, is one of the nation's largest financial services companies. It has a mission to be a trusted advisor to its clients and delivers a wide array of banking products for consumers and businesses. It is recognized among the top customer service providers.

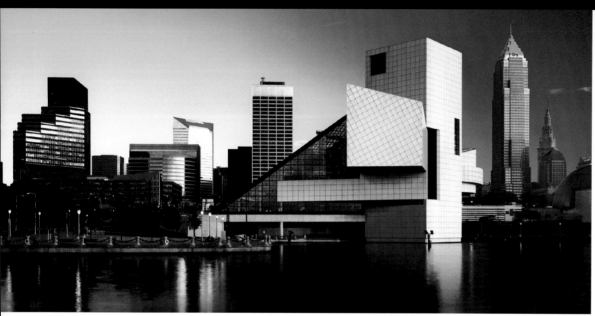

A Customer Service Champion

Every day, across the nation and abroad, Key's bankers offer ideas and products to help clients compete and succeed. In 2009 Key's relentless focus on service excellence made it the top-named bank on the *BusinessWeek* 2009 list of the Customer Service Champs in the United States.

What makes Key unique? The company emphasizes teamwork and taking ideas to clients. Deploying teams of experts who earn a trusted-partner relationship with clients, Key delivers a broad menu of banking products for consumers and businesses through more than 1,000 branches, a nationwide ATM network, and its award-winning Web site at Key.com. At the core, Key's approach to business is idea-oriented, client-focused, and teamwork-based.

The team approach is designed to ensure that clients have access to specialists who help them consider a range of alternatives and ideas. As a result, the company is one of the nation's largest bankers to small and mid-size companies. For individuals and families, Key offers sophisticated private banking and wealth management services in addition to cornerstone banking services.

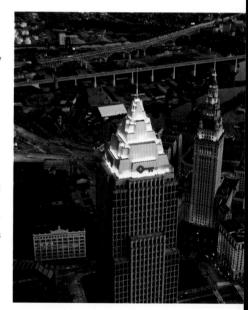

Key4Women

When Key recognized that significant numbers of new businesses were being started by women, it launched a multiyear initiative, Key4Women. With a goal of lending $2 billion to businesses owned by women, the company built partnerships with women's businesses and networks in communities where Key operates. Surpassing its original lending goal ahead of schedule, in 2009 the company announced an additional $3 billion in financing for women-owned businesses over the next two years.

As people come to know Cleveland, they discover that the city has far more business, cultural, sports, and recreational amenities than most U.S. cities of similar size. Some of the nation's largest and most influential financial services, health care, and manufacturing companies are headquartered in Cleveland. Among financial services firms, KeyBank parent KeyCorp is one of the nation's largest bank-based financial services companies, with approximately $100 billion in assets.

Key traces its roots to Society for Savings Bank of Cleveland, which was incorporated in 1849, and to 1825, when Commercial Bank of Albany, New York, was founded. Key's soaring headquarters building is a centerpiece of the Cleveland skyline. Today Key maintains branch banks and offices in locations from Portland, Maine, to Anchorage, Alaska. Its core mission is to be a trusted advisor to its clients.

Above and right:
KeyBank's Key Tower
is a familiar feature on
the Cleveland skyline.

Businesses that become Key clients find that the Key team of corporate bankers can offer cash management, asset management, equipment finance, foreign exchange, interest rate risk management, capital markets, and investment banking services. As a result, when companies grow and expand their facilities and distribution, they turn to Key for more complex products and for sound advice that extends far beyond the traditional bank loan. Key's business clients include many whose relationship spans decades and more than one family generation.

Community Is Key

Beyond its breadth of services and culture of teamwork and trust, Key also is known for its emphasis on community. Employees serve their communities through nonprofit organizations, churches, Little Leagues, and schools, as well as through economic-development organizations and United Way. Key employees today serve as members of boards of directors for thousands of nonprofit organizations around the nation.

Since 1990 Key's nationwide volunteer project, Neighbors Make the Difference Day, has provided a half-day off for employees, and thousands of them provide millions of dollars worth of "sweat equity" in communities across the nation. In addition, the KeyBank Foundation supports local and national programs dedicated to financial education, inclusion, and workforce development with funding, which exceeded $18 million in 2009

Through its KeyBank Plus program, an innovative approach to serving the community, Key provides check cashing and financial-education services to individuals who previously had no access to credit or a bank. This unique program—launched in

Cleveland in 2004 and now operating in 215 branch banks and offices around the nation—has become a model used by other banks, and was featured in a front-page article in *The Wall Street Journal*.

Emphasis on Diversity Earns National Recognition

Key develops its workforce to reflect the diversity of its clients and communities. In 2008 and 2009 the company was named to *DiversityInc* magazine's Top 50 Companies for Diversity for, among other efforts, its work/life balance, supplier diversity, and CEO commitment, and it received a special *DiversityInc* citation in 2007 as a Top 10 Company for Supplier Diversity. Key also has received perfect scores of 100 on the Human Rights Campaign Foundation's Corporate Equality Index.

Key Values—Trust and Relationships

Teamwork, respect, accountability, integrity, and leadership—these are the values by which Key's 17,000 employees live and the ways they support the bank's clients and communities. Henry L. Meyer III, KeyCorp chairman, president, and CEO, often points out, "Key is a relationship bank. This means that everything about our products and culture is designed around building long-term relationships with our clients and in our communities. At the end of the day, a customer's banking relationship is with individuals who have specialized skills and who approach their daily work with a set of values that we nurture every day, across the company."

KeyBank provides additional information about its products and services on its Web site at key.com.

Above left: A multiyear KeyBank program is adding dozens of new branches around the country and renovating about two-thirds of its 1,000 branch banks in 14 states. Above center and right: On Key's Neighbors Make the Difference Day, employees helped at Cleveland's Slavic Village (center) and in Vermont (right).

The PNC Financial Services Group, Inc.

One of the nation's leading providers of financial services, this Fortune 500 company has a wide national footprint and an international reach, yet remains committed to serving local customers and the communities in which it is established. Now, with the acquisition of one of the state's largest banks, it brings this same commitment to Northern Ohio.

The PNC Financial Services Group, Inc. is one of the country's leading financial institutions and the fifth-largest bank by deposits. It has achieved this status through customer-focused strategy based on offering the widest range of services to the broadest range of clients. PNC offers retail banking, wealth management, and corporate and institutional banking. Clients include individuals, the highly affluent, businesses of all sizes, educational and health care institutions, not-for-profits, and many others. Yet despite its size, PNC has remained true to the goal of its ancestor banks: to serve the local community, with leaders and decisions that are just as local.

Deep Community Roots

PNC was created in 1982 with the merger of two banks whose roots date back to the 19th century—Pittsburgh National Corporation and Provident National Corporation—and quickly expanded throughout Pennsylvania and into southern Ohio, Kentucky, Florida, New Jersey, Delaware, Maryland, and the District of Columbia. With the December 2008 acquisition of Cleveland-based National City, PNC became part of the Northern Ohio community.

National City itself was founded in 1845 as City Bank of Cleveland, serving the rapidly growing industrial community, which included such giants as Standard Oil and Sherwin-Williams. In 1865 it was chartered under the name National City Bank of Cleveland. The bank weathered the Great Depression and World War II and prospered in the 1950s and 1960s as it moved into the consumer market. It was the first national bank in the country to offer electronic check scanning and in 1962 became one of the first in the country to offer computerized savings deposits. The company continued to diversify and to acquire other banks, and in 1984 it became Ohio's largest bank. In 2000 it was converted to a financial services holding company. Further expansion followed, extending National City's reach into Cincinnati, St. Louis, Milwaukee, Chicago, and Florida.

With the acquisition of National City, PNC strengthened its portfolio of banks with a history of steadfast commitment to its customers, shareholders, employees, and communities. Today PNC serves more than six million customers in 15 states and the District of Columbia.

CORPORATE HISTORY HIGHLIGHTS

1845
City Bank of Cleveland, the local precursor of The PNC Financial Services Group, Inc., is established in Cleveland.

1918
National City acquires most of Guardian Trust's assets and its building.

1930
National City is the only bank in Cleveland to provide 100 cents on the dollar to customers during the Great Depression.

1940
National City offers Cleveland's first check-reconcilement services.

Services for Financial Success

PNC offers all its clients the knowledge, resources, and solutions they need to succeed. Its Retail Banking division provides some five million customers with a wealth of deposit, lending, cash management, and investment services, whether at one of its 2,600 branches or 6,000 ATMs or online. One of PNC's most innovative programs is Virtual Wallet℠, called "one of the boldest enhancements" in online banking by the international strategy consulting firm Celent. It provides a high-definition online view of a client's accounts and includes such features as online bill pay, a wish list, a savings engine, and a high-yield savings account.

PNC's Asset Management Group provides trust, private banking, tailored investments, and brokerage services to affluent individuals and families, while its Institutional Investments division serves as investment manager and trustee to businesses, retirement plans, and not-for-profit organizations. With approximately $120 billion in assets, PNC is ranked by *Barron's* as the nation's eighth-largest bank-held wealth manager.

The leading syndicator of middle-market loan transactions in the Northeast, PNC serves this segment through its Corporate and Institutional Banking division with treasury management, capital markets, and international banking services. The division also includes among its clients more than a third of Fortune 500 companies as well as thousands of real estate, education, health care, government, and not-for-profit institutions.

PNC also is part owner of Black Rock, providing institutional and individual investors with a variety of investment products.

PNC in the Community

The PNC Financial Services Group, Inc. will continue to grow with the Northern Ohio community through philanthropic outreach, economic development, and the volunteer efforts of its employees. PNC's signature philanthropic program is "Grow Up Great," a 10-year, $100 million initiative to help prepare children from birth to age five—with a focus on underserved children—for success in school and life. In Cleveland PNC already has committed $2 million through local partners, with further grants to come. Through its community development banking group, PNC boosts the quality of life in lower-income neighborhoods through affordable housing, economic revitalization, and customized financial solutions and education. PNC remains true to the strategies and policies that have made it both a global financial leader and a good local corporate neighbor.

Further information is available on the company's Web site at www.pnc.com.

Photo, far right: © Roger Mastroianni

1955
National City installs 24-hour night-depository services at each of its branches and retail stores.

2009
National City merges with The PNC Financial Services Group, Inc.

2009
PNC announces its first "Grow Up Great" grants in Cleveland to bolster early childhood education.

CBIZ, Inc.

This professional services company headquartered in Cleveland provides a comprehensive range of business services, products, and solutions designed to help its clients grow and prosper by optimally managing their finances and employees. Among the wide array of services it provides are accounting and valuation services, property and casualty and employee benefits consulting, medical practice management, and more.

Cleveland-based CBIZ, Inc. is a professional services company providing a comprehensive range of business services, products, and solutions that helps its clients grow and succeed. The company is one of the nation's leading

- Accounting Providers
- Employee Benefits Specialists
- Valuation firms
- Medical Practice Management firms

CBIZ has been operating as a professional services business since 1996, and built its professional services business through acquiring accounting, benefits, valuation, medical billing, and other service firms throughout the United States. Effective

August 4, 2006, CBIZ transferred the listing of its common stock to the New York Stock Exchange (NYSE) under the symbol "CBZ." Prior to August 4, 2006, CBIZ's common stock was traded on the Nasdaq National Market under the symbol "CBIZ."

With more than 150 offices and 5,500 associates in major metropolitan cities and suburban areas throughout the United States, CBIZ serves organizations of all sizes as well as individual clients across the nation. CBIZ's mission is to help clients grow and prosper by providing them with an array of high quality, professional services for businesses and individuals, with the first priority being to serve clients well. CBIZ's commitment to clients is on a par with the company's commitment to its associates and its focus on increasing value for shareholders. CBIZ maintains a professional culture that is supportive and motivating, fosters and rewards high performance, and creates meaningful career opportunities.

The services offered by CBIZ are organized by the company's client-centric philosophy, which denotes CBIZ's role as enabling clients to focus on their core competency while helping them better manage their finances and their employees.

In order to ensure regulatory compliance in the accounting industry, CBIZ is associated with Mayer Hoffman McCann P.C. (MHM) under an alternative practice structure, which legally separates the accounting and attest practice provided under the MHM brand from the tax practice and other financial services provided by CBIZ. The core services of CBIZ accounting include tax services and financial business consulting, while MHM services are focused on independent audit and attest services. Together, CBIZ and MHM are ranked as the nation's eighth-largest accounting provider and are positioned as a national alternative to the regional and national accounting firms.

In addition to accounting, financial services offered by CBIZ include valuation, assistance with mergers and acquisitions, medical practice management, wealth management, and health care consulting.

Through its Employee Services division, CBIZ offers employers a full spectrum of benefits services including group health benefit plan design, actuarial services, COBRA/Flex Administration, and a comprehensive online-benefits enrollment and administration system. Through its property and casualty and risk-management groups, the CBIZ Employee Services division offers personal and company insurance coverage.

In order to provide a wide range of employee-management services, CBIZ also offers nationwide payroll services; human resources (HR) services, such as HR outsourcing and compensation and recruiting services; as well as an array of retirement plan services.

There are few issues facing business owners and managers today with which CBIZ cannot assist. The wide array of services CBIZ offers is what makes the company unique, and the ability to help businesses with multiple needs is key to the success of CBIZ. The company's success can be measured in several ways. In the 13 years from 1996 to 2009, CBIZ grew from just over 400 associates in six offices to 5,500 associates in 150 offices nationwide and from 6,000 clients to more than 90,000. Annual sales increased from $27 million to more than $740 million, and earnings per share grew by at least 20 percent each year from 2003 through 2008.

In addition to expanding a successful business, CBIZ also embraces associate-enrichment programs, community service, and philanthropic initiatives. Through its CBIZ Women's Advantage program, which focuses on professional development, networking, skill-building, and recognition for its female associates, CBIZ works in partnership with Dress for Success (DFS) not only in Cleveland but also across the country. DFS promotes the economic independence of disadvantaged women by providing professional attire and career development tools. During DFS's annual fund-raiser in 2009, CBIZ donated more than $50,000 and 12,000 items of clothing to DFS affiliates nationwide.

CBIZ also proudly supports United Way of Greater Cleveland, Amateur Athletic Union (AAU) basketball, and Junior Achievement. Additionally, CBIZ encourages its associates to serve the community, as evidenced through the company's support of Business Volunteers Unlimited, and it has numerous associates who serve on the boards of directors of nonprofit organizations in northeast Ohio.

CBIZ, Inc. provides additional information about its services and products on its Web site at www.cbiz.com.

Left, both photos: CBIZ began trading on the New York Stock Exchange in 2006. Above right, both photos: CBIZ assists its community with financial donations to a variety of charities and by supporting the participation of its employees in the fund-raising activities and events of nonprofit organizations.

Dollar Bank

From its new Ohio headquarters in Cleveland, this venerable financial institution presides over a legacy of secure, solid, and steadfast management of its clients' funds. The nation's largest independent mutual bank*—with more than 60 branch offices, loan centers, and private banking centers throughout the Cleveland and Pittsburgh metropolitan areas— is committed to serving 'Main Street, not Wall Street.'

Above: Dollar Bank's Ohio headquarters in Cleveland features a magnificent 512-square-foot mosaic of the bank's iconic lion, which is visible from the street. This facility includes the headquarters branch, a private banking center, a training facility, and retail operational support.

Dollar Bank has prospered for more than a century and a half because it remains an innovator. In the 1970s Dollar Bank was the first bank to offer interest on checking accounts, and it pioneered telephone banking. In the 1990s the bank introduced its Online Banking and was chosen as one of the top 10 banks in cyberspace by The Money Page, an Internet consumer guide to banking and finance. On the heels of that recognition, the U. S. Treasury allowed Dollar Bank to be the first bank to offer savings bonds via the Internet. In 1998 Dollar Bank's Online Banking was selected for inclusion in the Smithsonian Institution's Permanent Research Collection as part of the *Computerworld* Smithsonian Innovation Collection.

Today consumers can stay up-to-date with their banking needs using a variety of on-the-go banking services, including Online Banking, Mobile Banking, and Text Message Banking.

Dollar Bank has also put cyber power to work specifically for business customers with CashAnalyzer®, a PC-based Internet money-management system that allows corporate customers to manage their money in real time, 24 hours a day. This innovative program—combined with other services like Positive Pay, Zero Balance Accounts, Lockbox, Check Imaging, Remote Deposits, and more—allows business customers to optimize their money management and minimize their risk.

In this age of mega mergers in the banking industry, Dollar Bank remains fiercely independent and committed to providing the highest-quality banking services to individuals and businesses for many years to come. As a mutual institution, it has no stock to sell. As a well-capitalized bank, it has no reason to sell. This means that consumers and businesses alike will continue to find Dollar Bank a viable option to meet their banking needs.

Dollar Bank has enjoyed three decades of serving the financial needs of the people and businesses of northeastern Ohio and has a unique understanding of their needs. Combining this understanding with the assets of a multibillion-dollar institution, the bank is well positioned to address those financial needs.

In business, experience matters. And it matters at Dollar Bank, too. Businessmen and businesswomen who come to the bank find themselves in the hands of tenured, hard-working banking officers backed by a team of financial experts. Many business customers have been working with the same team of banking officers for more than a dozen years. These Dollar Bank teams work virtually without walls to ensure that the best interests of the customer remain paramount.

Extending credit in the community remains the single most important aspect of Dollar Bank's efforts to meet the needs of its customers and communities.

Without credit, a community cannot grow and prosper. Dollar Bank's corporate and commercial real estate lenders work with local nonprofit organizations, government entities, and private borrowers to complete community development projects that spur job growth, enhance the tax base, and strengthen the community's economic viability. Recognizing this creativity, the Small Business Administration has designated Dollar Bank a Certified SBA Lender in order to help small entrepreneurs obtain the finances they need when they need them.

For more than 15 years, Dollar Bank has been given an "Outstanding" rating by federal regulators who analyze the bank's efforts to reinvest in the community. In addition to meeting the banking needs of its community, the bank strategically focuses its corporate giving on community development and neighborhood revitalization efforts. Supplementing the dollars that are contributed, the bank has an active Employee

Volunteer Program, which encourages Dollar Bank staff members to provide their time and expertise to projects and organizations that are of interest to them and their particular communities. The employees also have a hand in directing some of the bank's philanthropy when they supplement their own giving with the bank's Employee Gift Matching Program.

With assets topping $5.9 billion, Dollar Bank is the largest independent mutual bank in the United States,* operating 26 branches, two loan centers and two private banking centers in northeastern Ohio. Dollar Bank subsidiaries include Flenniken Settlement Services and the Dollar Bank Servicing Center.

At its core, banking has always been a business of responsibility and trust. The leaders of Dollar Bank feel an intense responsibility to provide products and services that grow out of an understanding of and feel for their communities. Customers trust that Dollar Bank will be there to meet their needs in the future.

Additional information can be found on Dollar Bank's Web site: www.dollarbank.com.

*Source: fdic.gov, mutual institutions as of 3/31/2010.

Above left: Dollar Bank operates more than 60 branch offices, loan centers, and private banking centers throughout the Cleveland and Pittsburgh metropolitan areas. Above right: Dollar Bank offers its customers the secure convenience of a full range of online banking services.

Fifth Third Bank

With roots dating back to 1858, today this nationally recognized, diversified financial services company provides commercial and consumer banking and investment services and manages electronic payment transactions for enterprises around the globe. Making major contributions through its foundation and neighborhood-development arm, the company continues its long-time commitment to supporting its communities.

Fifth Third Bank is a leading regional bank with 16 affiliates, located in 12 states. Since its beginning, Fifth Third Bank, headquartered in Cincinnati, has remained true to a philosophy of strength and stability. In 2009, for the eighth consecutive year, the company earned inclusion by *Fortune* among the magazine's top 10 in the Superregional Banks (U.S.) category of America's Most Admired Companies. The ranking is based on employee talent, social responsibility, innovation, quality of management, financial soundness, and long-term investment value.

Above: Fifth Third Bank's downtown Cleveland office is on Superior Avenue.

Fifth Third Bank, Northeastern Ohio, is the affiliate serving the eight-county area of greater Cleveland, Akron, and Canton and has served this area since 1992. Fifth Third associates are committed to focusing on customer relationships and on helping customers build their dreams to achieve a better tomorrow.

A Rich History, a Bright Future

Growth and innovation have been hallmarks of the company since its earliest days. Fifth Third traces its roots to the Bank of the Ohio Valley, started by 11 Cincinnati businessmen to serve the Ohio River trade. In 1871 the bank was purchased by the Third National Bank. In 1908 came the union of the Third National Bank and the Fifth National Bank, and eventually the organization became known as "Fifth Third Bank."

Today Fifth Third operates four main businesses: Commercial Banking, Branch Banking, Consumer Lending, and Investment Advisors. Fifth Third serves 5.8 million customers in 12 states, providing more than 1,300 full-service banking centers and 2,300 ATMs. Fifth Third is a diversified financial services leader assisting companies with their borrowing needs and providing a full spectrum of money-management options. Fifth Third also has a 49 percent interest in Fifth Third Processing Solutions, LLC, which authorizes and settles electronic payment transactions for well-known retailers and financial institutions around the world.

Giving Back to the Community

Fifth Third has a rich legacy of community support. In 1948 the bank became the first financial institution in the United States to establish a charitable foundation. Today it continues to invest the time, resources, and people to build a better tomorrow in the communities it serves.

In 2008 the Fifth Third Foundation awarded more than $30 million to worthy charities across the United States, supporting a variety of causes ranging from educational establishments to arts organizations and basic-needs, environmental, and animal-rescue efforts. The company's Community Development Corporation invests in housing and revitalization projects throughout local neighborhoods. Fifth Third's corporate and employee contributions to United Way totaled more than $7.6 million in 2008. Fifth Third Bank provides additional information on its Web site at www.53.com.

PROFILES OF COMPANIES AND ORGANIZATIONS
Health Care Services and Facilities

St. Vincent Charity Medical Center
A Ministry of the Sisters of Charity Health System

This award-winning, faith-based healthcare organization combines medical excellence with human compassion to provide comprehensive inpatient and outpatient healthcare. The medical professionals and physicians here pride themselves on treating the whole person.

can believe in, helping people to stay well and enjoy a lifetime of good health. The center's more than 1,200 dedicated physicians, nurses, and employees work daily to bring the healing ministry of Jesus to their patients and the Greater Cleveland community.

St. Vincent Charity Medical Center is an acute-care teaching hospital located in downtown Cleveland's Campus District. This 480-bed inpatient and outpatient healthcare facility offers a full range of medical and surgical specialties for adults as well as round-the-clock emergency care. The facility also provides a host of diagnostic services and clinics. Off-site facilities are located across Greater Cleveland, including locations in Solon, Brecksville, Church Square, Brookpark, and Independence, plus the former St. Luke's Medical Center in Cleveland.

Centers of Excellence at St. Vincent Charity Medical Center include the Joslin Diabetes Center, an affiliate of the world-renowned Joslin Diabetes Center at Harvard University. The Joslin Diabetes Center offers a collaborative approach and the latest research and advances in treating adults who have Type 1 or Type 2 diabetes.

The Center for Bariatric Surgery specializes in surgical treatment and support for the morbidly obese and has been named a Center of Excellence by the American Society for Metabolic and Bariatric Surgery. The center's experienced surgical weight loss team has helped more than 6,500 patients lose more than 650,000 pounds so far.

Above: Shown decorated in its winter finest, St. Vincent Charity Medical Center in Cleveland offers advanced, personalized healthcare in a compassionate environment.

St. Vincent Charity Medical Center has brought hope and healing to the Greater Cleveland community since 1865. Today St. Vincent Charity Medical Center continues its long legacy of service through its multiple centers of excellence and diverse spectrum of medical and surgical services. The compassion of its highly skilled and dedicated professionals is what truly defines St. Vincent Charity Medical Center. These individuals are passionate about providing care patients

At the Spine and Orthopedic Institute, the region's best surgeons use the latest technology and surgical innovations to provide top-notch care, treating injuries and chronic medical conditions of the neck, back, joints, and bones.

The Center for Vascular Health specializes in vascular research, medications, and treatments, providing comprehensive medical and surgical services for the diagnosis,

Photo: © Rob Wetzler

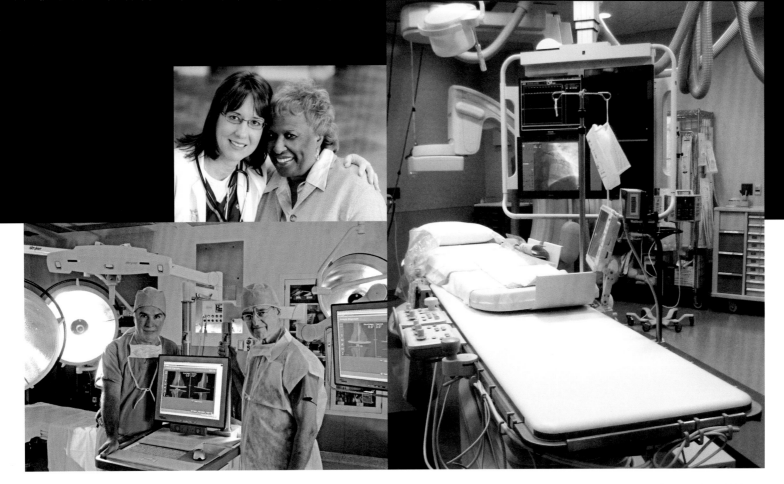

treatment, and prevention of heart and vascular diseases and conditions. Services include diagnostic testing, cardiac catheterization, open-heart surgery, and vascular medicine and surgery.

Other programs include Rosary Hall, which specializes in treating alcohol and drug dependency; Occupational Health, which specializes in work-related injuries; the Sleep Disorder Treatment Center, which diagnoses and treats sleep disorders; and the Geropsychiatry Program, which specializes in treating the psychiatric and medical needs of older adults.

St. Vincent Charity Medical Center is the recipient of numerous national awards and recognitions from HealthGrades, a leading independent healthcare ratings organization. Among its many awards, St. Vincent Charity Medical Center ranks among the top five medical centers in Ohio for spine surgery and achieved five-star ratings in both spine surgery and back and neck surgery. In addition, St. Vincent has received

five-star ratings for treatment of heart failure for eight years in a row, from 2003 through 2010. The patient-centered focus on quality has earned St. Vincent Charity Medical Center the HealthGrades Distinguished Hospital Award for Clinical Excellence™ for five consecutive years, from 2006 through 2010.

A New Era in Care

In December 2009, upon the completion of a transaction between the Sisters of Charity Health System and University Hospitals, the Sisters of Charity Health System regained complete ownership and governance of St. Vincent Charity Medical Center. At this time, the 145-year-old institution formerly known as St. Vincent Charity Hospital was reintroduced to the community as St. Vincent Charity Medical Center.

"This modest change to our name also reflects the teaching role of the hospital, which includes training physicians, dentists, podiatrists, and many other healthcare professionals for our community. This is further supported by our developing

Top left: St. Vincent Charity Medical Center employs more than 1,200 caregivers. The medical staff is composed of more than 300 physicians, encompassing primary care physicians, specialists, and surgeons who are devoted to providing clinical excellence and human compassion. Above right: St. Vincent Charity Medical Center received a five-star rating from HealthGrades in cardiac services for eight years in a row, from 2003 through 2010. Pictured is the new state-of-the-art catheterization laboratory. Above left: Louis Keppler, M.D. (left), and John Collis, M.D. (right), are the co-directors of The Spine and Orthopedic Institute at St. Vincent Charity Medical Center, which offers advanced medical and surgical care for the neck, back, joints, and bones.

Civil War. The organization continues to address many unmet community needs in Ohio and South Carolina by establishing hospitals, schools, and dozens of other health and social service programs. The institutional health and human service ministries of the Sisters of Charity of St. Augustine are overseen by the Sisters of Charity Health System (www.sistersofcharityhealth.org). The Sisters of Charity Health System is composed of:

- Five hospitals—St. Vincent Medical Center in Cleveland, Ohio; Mercy Medical Center in Canton, Ohio; St. John Medical Center in Westlake, Ohio (a joint venture with University Hospitals); and Providence Hospital and Providence Northeast, both in Columbia, South Carolina
- Three grant-making foundations—Sisters of Charity Foundation of Canton, Ohio; Sisters of Charity Foundation of Cleveland, Ohio; and Sisters of Charity Foundation of South Carolina
- Two elder care facilities—Light of Hearts Villa in Cleveland, Ohio (a partnership with Sisters of Charity of Cincinnati) and Regina Health Center in Richfield, Ohio
- Various community outreach ministries in Northeast Ohio and South Carolina

Faithful to the philosophy and heritage of the Sisters of Charity of St. Augustine, the St. Vincent Charity Medical Center family is committed to the healing mission of Jesus. As caregivers, the staff offers quality care, serving with a deep respect for the dignity and value of all persons, dedication to the poor, and a strong commitment to education.

"As when the Sisters of Charity of St. Augustine founded St. Vincent in 1865, our renowned physicians, nurses, and staff understand that true healing comes not only from advanced medical technology, but also from a warm, holistic, healing touch," says Karam.

A Bright Future

St. Vincent Charity Medical Center recognizes that high-quality patient care is best accomplished in exceptional surroundings. Several major renovations are planned for modernizing facilities at the center's main campus and areas in the surrounding neighborhood.

Above: St. Vincent Charity Medical Center's Solon Medical Campus provides excellent emergency care and award-winning treatment of heart failure, stroke, and pulmonary issues.

collaboration with Catholic Community Connection and also with our neighbors, Cleveland State University, Cuyahoga Community College, and the Campus District," says Sister Judith Ann Karam, CSA, president and CEO of the Sisters of Charity Health System and St. Vincent Charity Medical Center. "Yet it also remains true to our mission as an urban, faith-based hospital and our continuing quest for the highest-quality, patient-centered healthcare across our diverse service lines as well as our evolving role in promoting health and wellness."

The first Sisters of Charity of St. Augustine arrived in Cleveland in 1851 to serve as the city's first public health nurses. They went on to found the hospital in 1865 to serve the whole community, including soldiers returning home from the

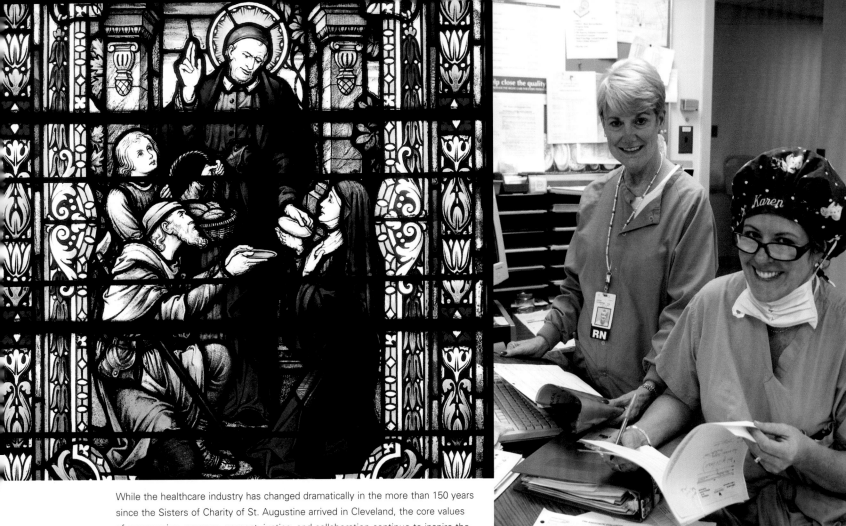

While the healthcare industry has changed dramatically in the more than 150 years since the Sisters of Charity of St. Augustine arrived in Cleveland, the core values of compassion, courage, respect, justice, and collaboration continue to inspire the work of St. Vincent Charity Medical Center. Additional information is available on St. Vincent Charity Medical Center's Web site at www.stvincentcharity.com.

Above left: Faithful to the philosophy and heritage of the Sisters of Charity of St. Augustine, the St. Vincent Charity Medical Center family is committed to the healing mission of Jesus. Above right: Caregivers at St. Vincent Charity Medical Center provide quality care and have a deep respect for the dignity and value of all persons.

The MetroHealth System

A regional leader in critical care, rehabilitation, and community and senior health care, MetroHealth has been caring for people in and around Greater Cleveland for more than 170 years. Affiliated with Case Western Reserve University School of Medicine, MetroHealth is an academic health care system committed to the communities it serves by saving lives, restoring health, promoting wellness, and providing outstanding, lifelong care that is accessible to all.

Above: The MetroHealth System's Critical Care Pavilion in Cleveland, opened in 2004, houses the community's largest emergency department and 20 of the most advanced surgical suites, including nine equipped for minimally invasive procedures.

Widely known as the public safety net health system with a unique mission and a deep commitment to the health of the community, The MetroHealth System provides comprehensive care with impressive quality outcomes in a wide range of specialties, from orthopedics and cardiology to women's health and pediatrics. Equipped with the area's largest emergency department, MetroHealth has pioneered innovative approaches to linking patients with primary care physicians to avoid expensive emergency visits and hospitalizations. This is part of the system's focus on keeping patients well, solving problems that impact their health, and managing costs so that high-quality medical care remains available to all, regardless of economic means.

With 12 outpatient health centers and specialty offices throughout Cuyahoga County, MetroHealth maintains a staff of highly trained physicians and nurses who deliver personalized care with compassion and dignity. MetroHealth has been nationally recognized for the quality of its care by organizations as prestigious as the American Heart Association, and it is among the nation's elite in achieving Magnet recognition, awarded by the American Nurses Credentialing Center to just six percent of hospitals

nationwide. MetroHealth's cancer center has earned outstanding achievement awards for the treatment of cancer patients. MetroHealth's surgeons are pioneering new techniques in minimally invasive surgery for faster recoveries. Its maternal-fetal medicine specialists are successfully managing the riskiest of pregnancies and saving even the tiniest babies. Its primary care physicians are developing innovative ways to manage common and chronic diseases through the use of electronic medical records and a patient-centered approach to care.

Heart and Vascular Care

MetroHealth's Heart and Vascular Center provides comprehensive cardiovascular services and is nationally recognized for its leadership in the diagnosis, treatment, and research of cardiovascular disease. This multidisciplinary center includes clinical cardiology, cardiothoracic surgery, vascular surgery, and the Heart and Vascular Research Center. The center places a strong emphasis on prediction, prevention, and treatment of heart disease using state-of-the-art technologies, evidence-based practice, and scientific discovery. MetroHealth has been recognized by the American Heart Association's Get with the Guidelines[SM] program for its highly successful approach to caring for patients with heart failure, coronary artery disease, and stroke. It is the first Cleveland hospital to receive a triple gold performance achievement award designation in all three categories.

Trauma, Critical Care, and Burn Care

MetroHealth's investment in life-saving technology, resources, and highly trained specialists makes it better equipped to save a person from critical injury or illness and restore quality of life than most other medical facilities in the region. The hospital is verified by the American College of Surgeons as a Level I Adult Trauma Center, and the Comprehensive Burn Care Center is verified by the American Burn Association. With more than 2,600 trauma admissions a year, the Trauma Center is one of the busiest in the nation. The 27-bed Surgical Intensive Care Unit admits more than 2,000 critically ill surgical patients per year. The Comprehensive Burn Care Center treats more than 1,700 outpatient and inpatient burn injuries annually.

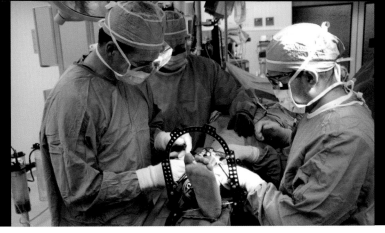

Orthopedics and Rehabilitation

MetroHealth's orthopedic surgeons lead the field in musculoskeletal trauma, hand surgery, and the treatment of spinal disorders, providing a full range of musculoskeletal services. Working in tandem with the MetroHealth Rehabilitation Institute of Ohio, the largest hospital-based rehabilitation program in the state and one of just 14 model systems nationwide in the care of spinal cord injury, MetroHealth's orthopedic surgeons provide patients with an outstanding choice for treatment and recovery. MetroHealth Rehabilitation Institute is also making remarkable advances in developing new technologies to improve patient care. For example, functional electrical stimulation (FES), developed at MetroHealth, Case Western Reserve University, and the Louis Stokes Cleveland VA Medical Center, restores movement in paralyzed patients. Paraplegic patients walk again; quadriplegic patients regain the use of their hands and arms and breathe without mechanical ventilation.

Maternal-Fetal Medicine

Very few hospitals have the comprehensive and specialized knowledge found at MetroHealth to help women deal with the unique health issues they and their families face during pregnancy and beyond. MetroHealth offers complete genetic evaluations and counseling for families with inheritable conditions that can put mother and child at risk. And during pregnancy, the reassurance that comes from the region's largest staff of maternal-fetal medicine experts is immeasurable. All women deserve the expertise of physicians who are nationally renowned for their work in high-risk pregnancy, diabetes in pregnancy, and premature delivery. MetroHealth delivers about 3,000 babies a year, and its Level III Neonatal Intensive Care Unit (NICU) has successfully treated some babies who weigh as little as one pound.

Senior Health and Wellness

The Senior Health & Wellness Center at MetroHealth's Old Brooklyn Campus is a model for the care of adults age 55 and older. The 354,000 square-foot campus includes MetroHealth's Senior Health Outpatient Program, a one-of-a-kind, one-stop shop for everything from primary senior care to specialty services, including cardiology,

dentistry, dermatology, mental health, neurology, podiatry, pulmonology, radiology, rheumatology, and ophthalmology. The Senior Health & Wellness Center has a unique, senior-focused approach to care, and its physicians are national leaders in their fields of expertise. The staff focuses on maintaining and improving the physical, emotional, and social well-being of seniors. Also housed in the center are a skilled nursing facility and an inpatient hospice unit operated by the Visiting Nurse Association.

Building a Medical Home

MetroHealth's emphasis on broadening access to primary care recognizes the importance of the relationship between physician and patient to manage chronic conditions like asthma and diabetes. The medical home concept, *Partners in Care*, also engages a team of nurses, medical assistants, and a care coordinator, among others, in creating a real support structure for each patient. The medical home model is designed to provide the right care at the right time, in the right place, especially for those with chronic conditions. It can reduce costs by minimizing patients' need for emergency care and hospitalization. MetroHealth *Partners in Care* medical home program helps patients form a healing relationship with their health care team.

A Tradition of Research and Education Excellence

Since its inception in 1837 and especially since its affiliation with Case Western Reserve University School of Medicine in 1914, MetroHealth Medical Center has been dedicated to the science of improving health care. All MetroHealth physicians hold academic appointments at the Case Western Reserve University School of Medicine and are frequently recognized as skilled teachers of the next generation of physicians. With $40 million a year in grant funding, MetroHealth researchers are focused on breaking new ground in many areas, including metabolic and kidney disorders, cardiology, and maternal-fetal medicine.

Additional information about MetroHealth and its locations and services can be found on the health care system's Web site at www.metrohealth.org. For remarkable patient stories of treatment and recovery at MetroHealth, visit www.mhwallofhope.com.

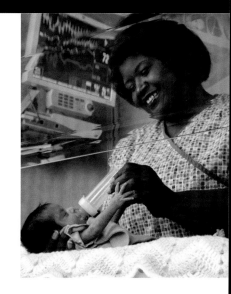

Top left: Named among the Best Doctors in America®, MetroHealth's orthopedic surgery team regularly performs limb-saving operations. Above right: The staff of MetroHealth's Neonatal Intensive Care Unit, certified to provide the highest level of care, has the expertise to save the tiniest babies and handle the most complicated births.

PROFILES OF COMPANIES AND ORGANIZATIONS

Manufacturing and Distribution

Preformed Line Products

Proudly headquartered in Mayfield Village, Ohio, this pioneer in power transmission creates groundbreaking and innovative solutions for the communications, energy, solar, and other specialized industries, providing the world with 'the connection you can count on.' With a staff of seasoned experts, exceptional customer support, flexibility, and a global presence, the company offers its customers reliability, efficiency, and value.

RESEARCH, ENGINEERING & DEVELOPMENT

COMMUNICATIONS   ENERGY   SPECIAL INDUSTRIES   SOLAR

company designs, manufactures, and supplies high-quality cable anchoring hardware and systems, fiber-optic and copper splice closures, and high-speed cross-connect devices for the communications, energy, solar, and special industries markets. PLP clients include power utilities, telecommunications network operators, cable television and broadband service providers, government agencies, educational institutions, and many others.

Client Solutions

In the 1950s PLP established its own Research and Engineering Center where it could simulate external conditions that affected its products. Today PLP's continued commitment to research and development allows the company to offer state-of-the-art products that fulfill every client's needs. For clients of the Communications Market group, PLP offers copper and fiber-optic products for connectivity and demarcation applications. Introduced in 2008, the COYOTE® Dome High Capacity Closure, LCC Closure, MPC Closure, and COYOTE In-Line RUNT Fire Retardant Closure allow increased bandwidth for Fiber-to-the-Premises networks. The group is also diversifying into the alternative energy sector. Its Axcess Solutions™ products and COYOTE Fiber Optic Closures are being used in monitoring and controlling grids whose power is provided by wind energy.

The Energy Market group serves the electric power utility industry with solutions for supporting, protecting, terminating, and splicing transmission and distribution lines. It also provides hardware for optical-ground-wire and all-dielectric-self-supporting fiber-optic cables used to monitor and control power networks. The alternative- and renewable-energy sectors are also fueling demand for PLP products, particularly for transmission use. Among PLP's latest transmission hardware items are the CUSHION-GRIP® Spacer Damper, the VORTX™ Vibration Damper, and the CUSHION-GRIP® Suspension Clamp.

In another example of the company's forward-thinking policies, in 2007 PLP acquired DPW Solar of Albuquerque, New Mexico, adding solar to its portfolio of

In the boom years that followed World War II, millions of miles of power lines were strung across the United States as the demand for more and better connections skyrocketed. Keeping those lines up and running was a challenge when adverse weather conditions and simple wear and tear took their toll. In 1947 Cleveland engineer Tom Peterson invented a device that would revolutionize the power industry: a preformed helical rod that fit over a conductor, securing the conductor without the need for hand-formed rods to protect it from fatigue and abrasion at suspension locations. Peterson called his invention the PREFORMED™ Armor Rod, and the company he founded became Preformed Line Products (PLP).

Today the innovative and entrepreneurial spirit that Peterson brought to his work inspires the researchers, management, field service personnel, and staff in PLP facilities around the world. Led by chairman, president, and CEO Robert Ruhlman—a 2008 Ernst & Young Entrepreneur of the Year® nominee—the

Above: Preformed Line Products provides innovative, high-quality, and reliable solutions that meet the rigorous demands of today's modern communications, energy, special industries, and solar networks.

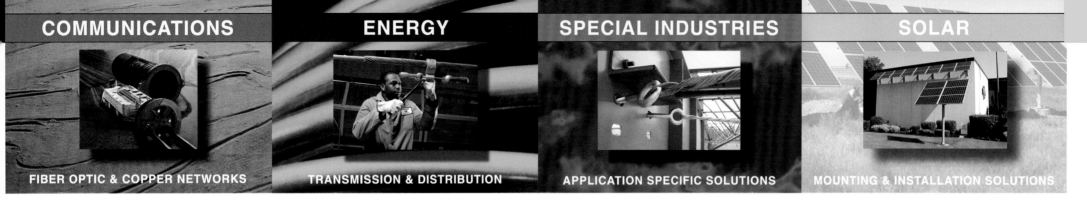

COMMUNICATIONS   **ENERGY**   **SPECIAL INDUSTRIES**   **SOLAR**

FIBER OPTIC & COPPER NETWORKS   TRANSMISSION & DISTRIBUTION   APPLICATION SPECIFIC SOLUTIONS   MOUNTING & INSTALLATION SOLUTIONS

power capabilities. DPW engineers design and install turnkey photovoltaic systems in homes, businesses, and industrial facilities and manufacture photovoltaic racks and equipment as well as battery enclosures.

PLP also creates specialized solutions for a wide range of other industries. Examples include the VARI-GRIP™ Dead-end for use in the construction of guyed structures that require a large guy strand such as towers and antennas. For the arborist industry, the WEDGE-GRIP™ Dead-end assists in tree-cabling installation. PLP also offers solutions for the agriculture, elevator, and residential-building industries. In addition, PLP provides a wealth of urethane product capabilities for the transit, mining, and rail industries.

Connecting Around the World

PLP's focus on research and development has allowed it to prosper even in difficult times. In 2008, as the world suffered an economic downturn, PLP posted net sales of nearly $270 million, a new record for the third consecutive year. The company is publicly traded on the Nasdaq National Market under the ticker symbol PLPC.

PLP is proudly headquartered in Mayfield Village, northeast of Cleveland. In addition to DPW Solar in New Mexico, the company has plants in Rogers, Arkansas,

and Albemarle, North Carolina, and international operations in Australia, Brazil, Canada, China, Indonesia, Malaysia, Mexico, Poland, South Africa, Spain, Thailand, and the United Kingdom.

Connecting in the Community

PLP's standards of excellence apply not only to its products and services but to its employees and to the community that has been its home for more than half a century. In 2008 the company was honored by the Office of Healthy Ohio, a division of the Ohio Department of Health, with the Healthy Worksite Silver Award for PLP's promotion of wellness programs and healthful practices at the workplace. The following year, PLP was the third-place winner (for companies with 101 to 250 employees) of the Wellness@Work Award, presented by the Cleveland Museum of Natural History, recognizing businesses for their health and sustainability programs. Also in 2009 PLP employees won the Champion Ohio Corporate Cup golf tournament, a fund-raiser for the Cleveland University Hospitals Rainbow Babies & Children's Hospital.

By consistently delivering the highest-quality products and services, Preformed Line Products will keep the world connected for generations to come. Further information on Preformed Line Products is available on the company's Web site, www.preformed.com.

Above, all images: PLP's core customer markets are divided into four distinct categories: communications, energy, special industries, and solar. The company's customer base includes telecommunications network operators, cable television and broadband service providers, power utilities, corporations and enterprise networks, government agencies, and educational institutions. PLP also serves several specialized areas through its special industries and solar market divisions.

Philips Healthcare

Dedicated to providing solutions designed around the needs of health care professionals and patients, this global health care leader combines human insights and clinical expertise to deliver the best possible products. Philips Healthcare strives to make a difference in people's lives by providing innovative and affordable technology solutions that will improve patient outcomes while lowering health care costs.

A Local Legacy

In Cleveland for more than 90 years, Philips Healthcare has been a leader in the medical imaging industry. In 1915 James Picker founded the Picker X-Ray Company in Cleveland, which quickly became a leading manufacturer of X-ray equipment with a national sales and supply network. In the 1950s the company expanded into nuclear medicine and industrial X-ray applications. In 1977 the company introduced the first computed tomography (CT) scanner, the first of many innovations developed by the company. Some other groundbreaking company developments include cobalt therapy for cancer, nuclear diagnostics, and the use of ultrasound for oceanography, which was then adapted for medical imaging.

The company was acquired by Royal Philips Electronics of the Netherlands in 2001 and became Philips Healthcare. The pioneering spirit of the original company continues today with inventions such as the Brilliance iCT, the fastest and most powerful CT scanner currently available globally. The Cleveland site is home to the largest Philips Healthcare division in the United States. It serves as the company's global headquarters for its computed tomography and nuclear medicine operations. The site also serves as the company's center for clinical education and service training. All of the activities needed for designing and manufacturing new medical imaging equipment are done here, from research and development to manufacturing and training the service engineers and the end user. The Cleveland location is also the site of the company's ultra high–field magnetic resonance imaging (MRI) research center, which features the Achieva 7.0T MRI whole body scanner, the first such machine installed in a corporate environment.

Philips Healthcare employs more than 1,100 people at its 44-acre Cleveland location, which includes three buildings. New technologies are designed and engineered in the laboratories, and service engineers are trained on the installation and service of the machines. Thousands of end users also travel to the Cleveland facility every year to be trained on the latest technology. "We are in an ideal environment in Cleveland," states Jay Mazelsky, the general manager of computed tomography and nuclear medicine

Above: The Philips Healthcare facility occupies approximately one million square feet of space in Highland Heights.

Health care is about people, and Philips Healthcare knows this well. To stay at the forefront of its quickly changing industry, Philips Healthcare pays close attention to the issues facing the imaging industry and the consequences of those issues. Then the company carefully formulates a solution—such as more efficient imaging tools, easily accessible digital images, and advanced capabilities—to meet each challenge. This process keeps Philips Healthcare ahead of the curve, allowing the company to provide health care professionals with the most advanced image acquisition technology and processing software, which fully supports the growth and evolution of their businesses.

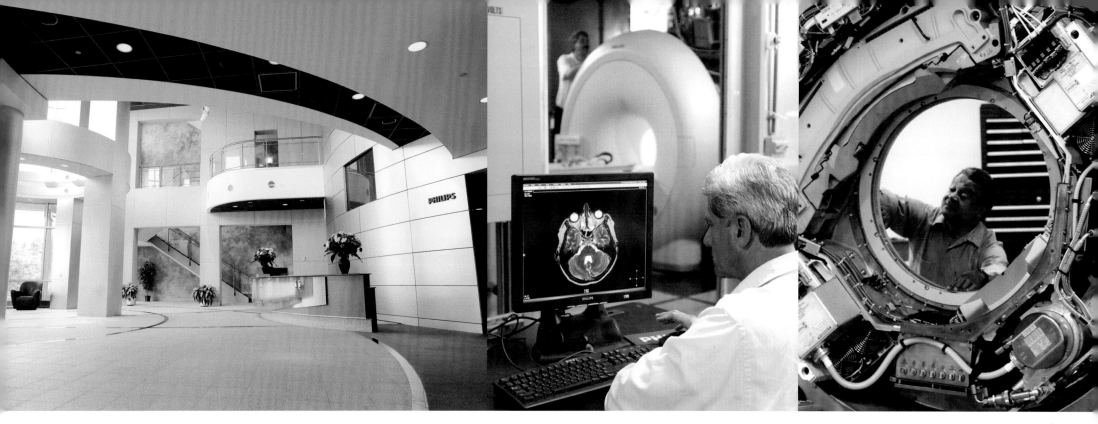

Photo, left: © Carl Fowler/Design Photography, Inc.

at Philips Healthcare. "Close proximity to some of the best health care institutions and prestigious universities in the nation gives us both the opportunity to do research and to develop new products that will advance health care in the future. We recruit the best talent for invention, manufacturing, product testing, research, clinical education, and service training with the continued goal of improving people's lives through better health care technology."

Global Reach

Royal Philips Electronics of the Netherlands, Philips Healthcare's parent company, is a diversified health and well-being company that is focused on improving people's lives through timely innovations. A world leader in health care, lifestyle, and lighting, Royal Philips integrates technologies and design into people-centric solutions based on fundamental customer insights and its brand promise of "sense and simplicity." Royal Philips employs approximately 118,000 people in more than 60 countries worldwide. The company is a market leader in cardiac care, acute care, and home health care; energy-efficient lighting solutions and new lighting applications; and lifestyle products for personal well-being and pleasure, with strong leadership positions in the flat-screen television, portable entertainment, male shaving and grooming, and oral health care industries.

People Focused

Philips Healthcare simplifies health care by focusing on the people directly involved in the care cycle—patients and care providers. The company is committed to developing tools that deliver value throughout the complete cycle of a patient's care—from disease prevention, screening, and diagnosis to treatment, health management, and monitoring—in key areas including cardiology, oncology, critical care, and women's health. By combining human insights and clinical expertise, Philips Healthcare aims to develop innovative solutions that improve patient outcomes at lower overall costs. Philips Healthcare's key business areas include imaging systems, home health care solutions, clinical care systems, and health care informatics.

Along with an unwavering innovative spirit, Philips Healthcare demonstrates environmental responsibility in all its business endeavors. Through its EcoDesign process, the company identifies the environmental impact of each new product in terms of energy efficiency, hazardous substances, recycling, weight, and lifetime reliability. A world leader in the health and well-being industries, Philips Healthcare is poised to continue its ascent in the business world through innovation and people-centric solutions. Additional information is available on the Philips Healthcare Web site at www.medical.philips.com.

Above left: Philips Healthcare's Customer Visitor Center at its Cleveland location hosts many guests from around the world. Above, center and right: Leading-edge medical technology is built right here in Cleveland. The world's first 7-tesla (7T) MRI scanner (center) and the fastest and most powerful CT scanner (right) are both built in Cleveland by Philips.

Energizer Holdings, Inc.

Best known for producing batteries promoted by the famous Energizer Bunny® and the 'keep going, and going, and going' tagline, this leading global consumer goods company offers products that people trust. From portable power, lighting, and personal grooming to skin, feminine, and infant care, goods manufactured by Energizer and its subsidiaries are found in households worldwide.

Energizer is all about taking care of people. A global leader in household and personal care products, Energizer Holding, Inc. makes products that deliver. Subsidiaries Energizer Battery, Schick-Wilkinson Sword, and Playtex are all pioneers in their industries, with commercial and production operations in 49 countries and distribution in another 131 countries.

A Rich Legacy

An integral part of Cleveland for more than 100 years, Energizer was formed in Cleveland as the National Carbon Company in 1886. Founder W. H. Lawrence bought the company's first facility on East 55th Street to produce open-arc carbons for street lamps, carbon brushes for dynamos, and porous plates for wet batteries. In 1890 the facility produced the world's first dry-cell battery.

In 1896 National Carbon introduced the 1.5-volt Columbia, the first dry battery produced and distributed to consumers on a large scale. Used to power telephones, the Columbia was so popular that the company built the first factory in the world devoted to dry-cell battery production.

In 1906 National Carbon purchased half interest in American Ever Ready, owned by flashlight inventor Conrad Hubert. The Cleveland company bought the remaining interest before becoming a part of Union Carbide Corporation in 1917. As the company expanded, its "Eveready" brand name became synonymous with power and reliability.

Charging Ahead

Over the course of several decades, the company continued to grow, focusing upon its strong reputation of producing "the dependable battery that you can trust." One of the company's young scientists knew that the product could be even better. In 1957 Lewis Urry developed a new battery with an extended life span powered by a chemical system now known as alkaline. Urry's invention was much more durable than the old carbon zinc batteries, and the company began production of the new battery. Since earlier batteries could barely provide enough power for a dimly lit flashlight, and then for only short periods of time, the alkaline battery was a major breakthrough. Eveready's alkaline battery laid the foundation for today's portable electronic devices.

In 1986 Ralston Purina bought Union Carbide's Battery Products Division to create Eveready Battery Company, Inc., now known by the name of its flagship brand, Energizer. Anticipating the trend toward high-tech equipment, Energizer continued to lead the industry in designing batteries to meet the power requirements of sophisticated electronic devices. Energizer was the first company to design and introduce a super-premium battery, and to harness the power of lithium in a commercially available

AA cell size. The company also revolutionized the rechargeable-battery category when it introduced a full line of high-powered Nickel Metal Hydride (NiMH) cells.

A Wide Range of Enduring Products

Energizer offers a complete portfolio of products designed to meet the needs of a wide range of consumers, including alkaline, carbon zinc, lithium, photo, miniature, and rechargeable batteries, as well as a complete line of flashlights and portable lighting products. The company's flagship brand, Energizer, offers premium, long-lasting battery performance that is constantly being improved. The company also offers a value brand, Eveready Alkaline, for consumers who seek a lower price and a brand name they can trust.

In addition to primary batteries, Energizer manufactures miniature batteries for hearing aids, watches, wireless remotes, and other devices. In the rechargeable battery sector, Energizer provides both round cells and power packs for portable electronics.

Energizer Holdings, Inc., created in 2000, is also the parent company of Playtex Products and Schick-Wilkinson Sword (SWS). Playtex is a maker of skin care, feminine care, and infant care products. Its brands include Banana Boat, Hawaiian Tropic, Wet Ones, Playtex gloves, Playtex tampons, Playtex infant feeding products, and Diaper Genie. SWS is the world's second-largest manufacturer of wet-shave products, including men's systems, women's systems, and disposables.

Cleveland as Energy Central

Energizer has two key locations in Cleveland, the Energizer Global Technology Center in Westlake and a global manufacturing facility in Garrettsville. Opened in 1982, the 235,000-square-foot Energizer Global Technology Center houses research and development operations, supporting work that ranges from fundamental studies in electrochemistry, material science, polymer science, and related sciences to the development of specific battery designs and unit operation processes for automated, high-speed battery manufacturing. Each operation is performed by a specific group

of individuals who are assigned to particular battery sizes and electrochemical systems. The Westlake facility also houses a number of supporting services, such as equipment engineering, which provides mechanical engineering and machine-shop services to fabricate battery parts and components; analytical laboratories, which provides a full complement of diagnostic and analytical instrumentation; a technical information center, Energizer's worldwide centralized resource for technical and business information about batteries and related communities; and battery applications and devices groups, which provide operational profiles for battery-operated devices, build specialized equipment, conduct battery testing, and consult on battery applications and design.

A Pioneer in Sustainability

Energizer is committed to preserving the environment for future generations. The company has always taken proactive steps to minimize the impact of its products and manufacturing processes on the environment, and it continues to research ways to improve these measures. Energizer has led the industry in eliminating heavy metals from its batteries while improving performance. In the 1990s, Energizer introduced the first zero-added mercury battery in the United States. Today the company produces hearing aid batteries with no added mercury. The company also offers long-lasting and rechargeable batteries. Even the company's packaging materials for the products are recyclable in areas where recycling is available to help the environment.

Always a forerunner in innovation, Energizer will continue to lead the way in its dynamic industry. Energizer is proud to bring convenience and portability to people's lives and is dedicated to producing top-quality products with minimum impact on the environment. Additional information is available on the company's Web site at www.energizer.com.

Above: Energizer is recognized not only for its products but also for its marketing techniques. Its Energizer Bunny® made its first appearance in 1989, marching across television screens in flip-flops and sunglasses, banging a drum. Consumers quickly got the message that these batteries "keep going and going and going." Since that time, the Energizer Bunny has become a pop icon. Here, children help him celebrate his 20th birthday in 2009 in Westlake, Ohio.

Eaton Corporation

Committed to delivering the innovative solutions and clean technologies companies need to manage energy and conserve resources, this Cleveland-based technology leader is expanding its presence around the world. Nearly 100 years in business confirm the company's commitment to combine its drive for performance excellence with its dedication to doing business right.

Powering Business Worldwide

Right: At Cleveland's Voinovich Park, Eaton Corporation—working with UPS and the U.S. Environmental Protection Agency—unveils a new hybrid hydraulic diesel truck technology that saves energy and reduces emissions. Eaton is a global leader in hybrid technology for commercial vehicles. Far right: A group of Eaton employees paint outdoor structures at Hiram House Camp in Chagrin Falls during the company's annual two-day United Way "Days of Caring" event.

Eaton Corporation, a global Fortune 500 company, helps clients use power more efficiently. The company develops systems and components for the aerospace, automotive, electrical, hydraulic, and truck industries. With 2008 sales of $15.4 billion and a global team of 70,000, Eaton moved up an impressive 43 spots on the 2009 Fortune 500 list to number 164.

The company makes important things work, as evidenced by its client list. Global industry leaders such as Airbus and Caterpillar, Shell and Volkswagen, rely not only on the innovative solutions Eaton brings to the table but on the company's unwavering commitment to sustainability and ethics.

To better provide the power systems today's markets require, Eaton reorganized its five business segments into two in 2009. The Electrical Sector—Eaton's single largest business, with 2008 sales of $6.9 billion—serves the mission-critical industrial, utility, commercial, residential, and information technology markets. Its products include power distribution, uninterruptible power supply, and industrial automation systems. Organized into "Electrical Americas" and "Electrical Rest of World," this sector is now positioned to accelerate Eaton's growth on a regional scale. The newly formed Industrial Sector combines Eaton's aerospace, hydraulics, truck, and automotive operations, streamlining development and expanding its capacity to offer integrated solutions. This combined $8.5 billion sector also provides technology for just about every power use, from vehicles to infrastructure. Among the products emerging from this sector are conveyance, fuel, and sensing and control systems (aerospace); fluid conveyance, power, and filtration systems (hydraulics); clutches and transmissions (truck); and power train systems, superchargers, and fluid connectors (automotive).

Just two years after Joseph O. Eaton founded Eaton Corporation in New Jersey in 1911, he moved it to Cleveland, Ohio, where it has been based ever since. Today Eaton has seven other locations in the Cleveland area in addition to its headquarters: the North American Financial Services Center in Brook Park, Telecomputer Center in Eastlake, an electrical facility in Parma, Learning and Technology Center in Willoughby, and manufacturing facilities in Brooklyn, Euclid, and Aurora.

Early on, Joseph O. Eaton joined Cuyahoga County community leaders in supporting local social service organizations. This effort became the United Way—and the beginning of a long tradition of community service and values-based business at Eaton Corporation. To learn more about this company, please visit its Web site at www.eaton.com.

ENPAC LLC

The world leader in proprietary spill containment, this privately owned, Eastlake-based company has for more than 20 years produced polyethylene spill containment products that set the standard for the industry. These high-quality, value-driven products ensure worker safety, support the customer's bottom line, and help protect the environment.

Above left: ENPAC LLC was honored with *Inside Business* magazine's 2009 Manny Award for green initiative for its Storm Sentinel filter, which traps chemicals and debris before they run into rivers, lakes, and the water supply. Company principals Scott Janda (left), vice president of business development, and Tim Reed (right), chief financial officer, are shown. Above, all other images: ENPAC designs and manufactures proprietary spill-containment products at its Molding Technology Center and headquarters in Eastlake, Ohio, near Cleveland.

On the earth's southernmost continent, scientists at the British Antarctic Survey station refuel their snowmobiles and inshore inflatables using the ENPAC® Poly-Dolly, which minimizes spills and leaks, preventing ground pollution and saving precious fuel. In the Middle East, Israeli Army personnel practice fuel handling using the ENPAC® Stinger Containment Berm, which offers rapid deployment and material safety. In Northern Europe, a rescue team from the Helsinki police removes a letter suspected of containing anthrax by putting it in an ENPAC® Overpack Salvage Drum.

These are but a few examples of the global impact of ENPAC LLC. The company is the world's largest producer of plastic spill prevention, containment, and control products. Distributed in more than 50 countries, ENPAC's innovative and award-winning products meet and exceed the most rigorous industry and government standards and are recognized around the world for their quality, durability, and value.

ENPAC debuted in 1989 with its signature Poly-Overpack® Salvage Drum designed to meet specific government regulations. Still one of the company's most popular items, the drum is featured in ENPAC's comprehensive catalog, which includes products for dispensing, storage, and portable containment; sorbents; spill kits; funnels; cylinder products; and much more.

As a leader in hazardous materials containment, ENPAC plays an important role in the green movement. Among its recent innovations is the Storm Sentinel filter, for which ENPAC was honored with *Inside Business* magazine's 2009 Manny Award for green initiative, recognizing excellence in manufacturing. Installed in storm drains, the Storm Sentinel prevents oil and debris from flowing into the water supply. It is one of 50 new products introduced in 2009, and ENPAC currently has more than 20 new products slated for a 2010 release.

As with its products, ENPAC continues to grow as a company, experiencing 10 percent growth nonstop since 1998. In addition to its manufacturing plant and headquarters in Eastlake, Ohio, ENPAC has distribution centers in Belgium, Australia, Peru, South Africa, Israel, and Singapore and in 2009 established ENPAC ASIA in Shanghai, China. Fully 30 percent of company sales come from international operations.

ENPAC may have a global reach, but it is firmly committed to the northeastern Ohio community it calls home. The company's many philanthropic pursuits involve contributions to or participation in such organizations as the American Heart Association, the American Cancer Association, and United Way; Boy Scouts and Girl Scouts of America; the Make a Wish Foundation; Catholic Charities; and local educational and other institutions. Additional information is available on the company's Web site at www.enpac.com.

ENPAC is a registered trademark of ENPAC LLC

Plastic polymer pellets such as the ones pictured above
are used in ENPAC's spill containment products.

Sysco Cleveland, Inc.

Helping its customers create healthful, appetite-pleasing menus that keep their dining patrons loyal, this subsidiary of food service giant Sysco Corporation provides everything necessary to prepare meals away from home. Using advanced technology, top-quality foods and equipment, and a highly efficient distribution system, Sysco Cleveland helps ensure the continued success of its customers.

Northeast Ohio's largest distributor of food service products and restaurant supplies, Sysco Cleveland, Inc. is dedicated to helping its customers succeed. A wholly owned subsidiary of Sysco Corporation, the largest food service distributor in North America, Sysco Cleveland distributes fresh and frozen meat, poultry, seafood, fruits and vegetables, canned and dry products, paper and disposable products, cleaning supplies, kitchen equipment, and fresh produce. Customers include restaurants, schools, hotels, health care institutions, and other food-service operations.

Parent company Sysco Corporation was formed in 1969, when several independent food-service distributors merged. Shortly after its founding, Sysco began to acquire additional distributors that shared Sysco's philosophy of "helping its customers succeed." Sysco Cleveland—which was started in 1967 by Jack Reasoner as the Cleveland division of The Miesel Company of Detroit, Michigan—began as one of those acquisitions. In 1972 The Miesel Company merged with the newly formed Sysco Corporation. While organic growth has been a key part of Sysco Cleveland's growth strategy, several acquisitions have also fueled its growth, necessitating several moves to larger facilities over the years.

In the beginning, Sysco Cleveland was primarily focused on dry grocery products, since distribution of nonperishable items was simple and did not require costly refrigerated delivery vehicles. Since then Sysco Cleveland has expanded its

product offerings into everything a restaurant, hotel, school, hospital, or long-term care facility needs to provide meals to its customers. Sysco Cleveland stocks and makes daily deliveries of anything a food-service operator wants and needs, from produce, milk, eggs, and meat to coffee, vegetables, soups, and desserts. As a broadline food-service distributor, Sysco Cleveland even provides the plates, glasses, and cutlery as well as the products to clean and wash everything.

Sysco Cleveland moved to its current site in Cleveland in August 2004. The location near Hopkins Airport was desirable because of its proximity to the Cleveland highway system and to the company's employee and customer base. Centered on 49 acres, Sysco Cleveland's state-of-the-art facility—engineered to be as environmentally friendly as possible—was designed for efficiency and future growth and is able to operate under any conditions. The facility is composed of a multi-temperature distribution center, a truck maintenance facility, an automated truck wash facility, and a fueling center. A modern fleet of more than 100 multi-temperature trucks are dispatched daily throughout Northeast Ohio to ensure that Sysco Cleveland's customers get what they want, when they want it, at the proper storage temperature.

Additional information about Sysco Cleveland, Inc. is available on the company's Web site at www.syscocleveland.com.

Above, all photos: Located in a new state-of-the-art distribution facility on Cleveland's West Side, Sysco Cleveland, Inc. serves customers across a range of industries.

Good things come from

PROFILES OF COMPANIES AND ORGANIZATIONS

Real Estate Services

Developers Diversified Realty Corporation

Headquartered in Beachwood, Ohio, this award-winning company owns, develops, and manages a dynamic portfolio of highly valued shopping centers in nearly every state, plus Puerto Rico and Brazil, creating experiences that delight shoppers and enhance quality of life. It is committed to supporting its local communities.

public company expanded rapidly through acquisitions and joint-venture partnerships, while honing strategies that dominate current business priorities for shopping centers: foster organic growth and a healthy tenant base at every property, maintain a diversified portfolio of tenants, and continue to align with the best strategic partners.

Complementing Developers Diversified's key strategies is the driving determination to occupy prime locations. In community after community, the company's shopping centers are situated in well-populated locations with ample household incomes, outstanding access, and competitive advantages. The company that has risen to become the industry leader it is today—with prominent shopping centers in nearly every state plus Puerto Rico and Brazil—is led by a talented team that is deeply experienced in commercial real estate, specifically the development and management of shopping centers. The executive team's passionate commitment to the company, its shareholders, and its employees is evidenced by team members' tenure, not only in the shopping center industry but within the company as well. The average tenure of executive members of management exceeds 12 years with the company and 20 years in the shopping center industry.

Community centers anchored by Wal-Mart, Target, Kohl's, and other high-profile retailers characterize Developers Diversified properties, but the company also has come to excel in developing mixed-use, lifestyle, and hybrid centers, and in redeveloping once-thriving malls and shopping centers to best meet today's demands and opportunities. As a result, the portfolio of Developers Diversified includes dynamic shopping centers carved out of urban cores, former malls that have been extensively renovated and renewed to regain prominence as shopping hubs, and expansive shopping centers with central parks and scenic walking trails that quickly become community gathering spots.

In addition to demonstrating its diversity by custom-developing shopping center formats to meet the needs of the consumer and retailer, Developers Diversified is an industry leader in ancillary income and marketing initiatives. By recognizing that each shopping center is much more than a collection of stores, Developers Diversified has

Above: Developers Diversified Realty Corporation's Plaza del Sol, a 675,000-square-foot enclosed regional mall, is the dominant shopping destination in the city of Bayamon, an inner suburb of San Juan, Puerto Rico.

Since its creation in 1965 by the late Bert L. (Bart) Wolstein, Developers Diversified Realty Corporation has been groundbreaking and forward-thinking while never straying from its founding commitment to give shoppers value and convenience. The early community shopping centers that dotted the country and today's portfolio of diverse formats may seem to have little in common, but they have all been born of a strict guiding principle: offer consumers the most prominent retailers, while being willing to innovate to take advantage of shifting business conditions and new shopping trends.

In 1993, under the direction of Scott A. Wolstein, the company entered a new era when Developers Diversified Group became Developers Diversified Realty Corporation and began operating as a real estate investment trust (REIT). The new

generated income and higher visibility through the innovative use of existing internal and external spaces. The company's imaginative marketing efforts are frequently honored with the International Council of Shopping Centers' MAXI Awards.

Developers Diversified is a multiyear recipient of the Employers Resource Council (ERC)'s NorthCoast 99 award, which honors great workplaces from Northeast Ohio. Developers Diversified is recognized as one of the area's top workplaces for its efforts in attracting, motivating, and retaining outstanding performers. The company invests extensively in giving employees abundant opportunities to realize their potential and advance within the organization. It also provides employees with a supportive work environment. Two prominent examples of this are a highly regarded management training program, which grooms promising college graduates for leadership roles through rotations in various operating departments, and the women's initiative program, which provides sessions on career advancement that are combined with social, recreational, educational, and community service opportunities.

Developers Diversified's deep commitment to acting responsibly is reflected at its corporate headquarters in Beachwood, Ohio, and across the nation. Locally, the desire to give back is manifested in company and employee support of organizations such as the National Multiple Sclerosis Society, Susan G. Komen for the Cure, The Gathering Place cancer support center, the YWCA, the Great Lakes Science Center, United Way, the Cleveland Foodbank, and many more. At its myriad properties, Developers Diversified's values take form in countless contributions to local communities—many involving activities at the company's shopping centers.

Likewise, to benefit the environment, the company is taking increasing steps in Beachwood and throughout the United States at the various locations of its assets and satellite offices, thereby demonstrating significant strides toward environmental sustainability across the nation. One significant example is at the three-building Developers Diversified campus in Beachwood, where information technology initiatives are enabling the company to become paperless. The company is also reusing building materials in new construction, employing methods of water conservation, and installing solar panels on shopping center rooftops.

Developers Diversified is dedicated to enhancing shareholder value by being the most admired provider of retail destinations. Its steadfast aspirations are supported by its continuing emphasis on central ideals, such as innovation, integrity, teamwork, and tenacity, which enable it to encourage the talents of employees, create new growth opportunities, and exceed the expectations of customers. Developers Diversified Realty Corporation provides additional information on its Web site at www.ddr.com.

Developers Diversified has shopping centers in nearly every state plus Puerto Rico and Brazil. Top left: In Manaus, Brazil—one of the country's fastest-growing cities—Manauara Shopping features a unique design that incorporates the natural elements of the Amazon region. Top right: In Miami, Florida, The Shops at Midtown Miami is a 645,000-square-foot mixed-use shopping center located just north of downtown Miami, adjacent to the Miami Design District. Above left: About 30 miles south of Miami, Homestead Pavilion is a 360,000-square-foot community center including Kohl's, Ross Dress for Less, Sports Authority, PETCO, Michaels, Staples, Bed Bath & Beyond, specialty shops, and restaurants.

PROFILES OF COMPANIES AND ORGANIZATIONS
Transportation

Cleveland Airport System
Cleveland Hopkins International Airport and Burke Lakefront Airport

Celebrating more than 85 years of 'going places,' the Cleveland Airport System—which includes Cleveland Hopkins International Airport and Burke Lakefront Airport—offers safe and efficient air service and world-class hospitality in its clean and welcoming facilities. Northeast Ohio travelers and businesses are served well by these historic yet cutting-edge airports.

Right: Cleveland Municipal Airport, now Cleveland Hopkins International Airport (CLE), was the first municipally owned commercial airport in the United States when it opened in 1925. Today CLE is the largest commercial airport in Northeast Ohio, serving almost 10 million passengers annually. Far right: William Hopkins, city manager and founder of Cleveland Municipal Airport, and American aviation pioneer Amelia Earhart pose together at the first-ever national air races held in Cleveland in 1929. In honor of William Hopkins, the airport name was changed to Cleveland Hopkins Airport in 1951.

Cleveland has a rich aviation history. The city is credited with many firsts in flight, from attracting first-rate aviators hosting the National Air Races from 1929 to 1949 and the opening of Aircraft Engine Research Laboratory in 1941 (now NASA Glenn) to numerous advancements in aircraft technology developed by Eaton Corporation, Parker Hannifin Corporation, and TRW Inc.

Cleveland Hopkins International Airport (CLE) shares in this innovation. It was the country's first municipally owned airport when it opened in 1925. Initially, the airport served as a stop for U.S. Air Mail planes making coast-to-coast flights. It quickly

grew to become a major destination for personal and commercial aircraft. CLE also led the nation in implementing new airport technology, including the world's first radio-equipped air traffic control tower and the nation's first airfield lighting system. In 1968 CLE became the first to offer direct rail service from an airport terminal to a downtown area, with a new connection via the Greater Cleveland Regional Transit Authority (RTA) Red Line Rapid Transit Service.

Today CLE continues to be a leader in aviation. It remains one of the only commercial airports in the United States connected to a major NASA facility. Green thinking has also become a top priority, with the airport exploring new ways to protect the environment, such as its de-icing reclamation system. This advanced system collects de-icing runoff to prevent ground water contamination. It also speeds up ground clearance time, with the capacity to simultaneously de-ice six Boeing 737 aircraft and two regional jets.

In the area of safety and security, CLE has implemented a state-of-the-art Emergency Operations Center. It also continues to receive exceptional ratings from the Federal Aviation Administration for runway safety.

Geographic location makes CLE an important gateway for air travel. It is positioned within 500 miles of 43 percent of the U.S. population. Just 12 miles away from downtown Cleveland, the airport is conveniently located for Northeast Ohio travelers.

CLE is Ohio's busiest airport, serving 10 million passengers and accommodating 200,000 flight take-offs and landings every year. Much of the airport's traffic is carried by Continental Airlines, which has made CLE one of its three hubs. Eight other carriers also operate out of CLE. Combined, the carriers make more than 250 daily nonstop flights to more than 70 destinations around the world.

Airports not only allow people to go places, they advance the cities they serve. CLE is a hub for economic growth, bringing $3.5 billion to the Northeast Ohio economy and supporting more than 34,000 jobs. And for major Cleveland area businesses, CLE is a lifeline to customers, suppliers, and subsidiary operations located in the United States and around the globe.

CLE is not Cleveland's only airport. Burke Lakefront Airport (BKL) is also vital to the local economy. This strategically located general aviation airport relieves CLE of corporate, charter, and personal aircraft traffic, minimizing flight delays. Annually BKL records nearly 70,000 takeoffs and landings. The airport has become key to Northeast Ohio's growing medical industry, providing the Cleveland Clinic,

University Hospitals, and MetroHealth with a nearby air-service hub for out-of-state patients, organ donations, and medical specialists.

The FAA is expected to approve BKL's master plan in the near future. The changes proposed in the plan will enhance safety and improve flight operations. Complementing this plan is a lakefront development proposal that includes the creation of retail shops, restaurants, and office space, capitalizing on BKL's premier location and proximity to the Rock and Roll Hall of Fame and Museum.

CLE is going through its own renaissance. The airport is enhancing the traveler's experience, from providing free Wi-Fi service and curbside valet parking to offering a cell phone waiting lot, where motorists meeting arriving passengers can wait for free until passengers call to say they are ready to be picked up. Work has also begun on the installation of terrazzo flooring that incorporates artwork images of Cleveland.

Among the enhancements garnering the highest marks by customers is the new AIRMALL®. It brings together well-known national brands and high-quality local concepts to provide passengers with the best retail, food, and beverage offerings. Equally as important, the merchants operating in the AIRMALL must sell goods at or below regular mall prices found outside the airport. When complete, the AIRMALL will offer 76,000 square feet of food and retail venues.

Celebrating its 85th anniversary in 2010, CLE has been a destination for billions of travelers. It has welcomed home Clevelanders, launched businesses, and intro-duced many aviation firsts. It is now poised to go new places to take customer service to new heights. Additional information about CLE and BKL can be found on Cleveland Airport System's Web site at www.clevelandairport.com.

CLE provides travelers with a wide variety of retail stores and eateries. Above left: The Rock and Roll Hall of Fame and Museum store pays homage to Cleveland's hometown treasure. The store features clothing, Hall of Fame memorabilia, gifts, and accessories. Above right: The Hudson News Euro Café offers travelers sandwiches, salads, coffee, and freshly prepared baked goods from Fragapane's, a popular Cleveland bakery. It also features a wide selection of newspapers, magazines, books, tobacco products, snack foods, and travel accessories.

PHOTO CREDITS

cherbo publishing group, inc.

TYPOGRAPHY

Principal faces used: Univers, designed by Adrian Frutiger in 1957; Helvetica, designed by Matthew Carter, Edouard Hoffmann, and Max Miedinger in 1959

HARDWARE

Macintosh G5 desktops, digital color laser printing with Xerox Phaser 7400

SOFTWARE

QuarkXPress, Adobe Illustrator, Adobe Photoshop, Adobe Acrobat, Microsoft Word, Eye-One Match by X-Rite, FlightCheck by Markzware

PAPER

Text Paper: #80 Luna Matte

Bound in Rainbow® recycled content papers from Ecological Fibers, Inc.

Dust Jacket: #100 Sterling-Litho Gloss